Y0-DOL-591

# *Journey*
## to
# JOY

*Love & joy!*

♡ *Elona Shelley*

## ALSO BY ELONA K. SHELLEY

*Confessions of a Molly Mormon:*
*Trading Perfectionism for Peace,*
*Fear for Faith, Judging for Joy*

# Journey to JOY

### Rising Above the Clouds of Perfectionism

## ELONA K. SHELLEY

sΔp
Summit View Publishing
Orem, Utah

Cover image Beautiful Sky (#11586368) by Deklofenak © Royalty-Free/DepositPhoto
Names and details have been changed to protect the privacy of individuals.

© 2018 Elona K. Shelley

All rights reserved. No part of this book may be reproduced in any manner or form without written permission from the author. The views expressed herein are the responsibility of the author and do not necessarily represent the position of The Church of Jesus Christ of Latter-day Saints.

Summit View Publishing
Orem, Utah 84097
www.SummitViewPublishing.com or www.sviewp.com

ISBN-13: 978-0-9818692-8-5
ISBN-10: 0-9818692-8-9

Printed in the United States of America
10 9 8 7 6 5 4 3 2 1

This book is printed on acid free paper.

To my dearly beloved family.


Each of you has contributed
something precious
to my journey and
I adore you one and all.

# CONTENTS

# ACKNOWLEDGMENTS

I am filled to overflowing with gratitude for the countless people who have helped this book come to be. It has evolved significantly through time and edits and is now a far cry from the fledging manuscript that poured from my pen over ten years ago. I am particularly indebted to my beloved husband, Monte, who has patiently stood by me in this endeavor, encouraging me and supplying his expertise whenever and wherever needed. I am likewise indebted to my amazing daughter, Christina Shelley Albrecht, who has been my first-draft editor, as well as consultant/editor on every other draft along the way. She has been my confidant, my cheerleader, my coach, and my inspiration. This project would have been much more difficult without her endless support. I also owe a huge debt of gratitude to my son, David, who has encouraged my efforts to complete this book. He has very possibly been my greatest teacher in life as we have navigated our challenges together.

My debt of gratitude certainly extends to the many friends, family members, and acquaintances who have taken the time to read drafts of this book and respond with comments and suggestions. It is a labor of love that money cannot buy. Their kind and encouraging words have sweetened the laborious task of finishing all the details required for publication. It is an honor to associate with so many supportive and generous people.

Amy Hardison, Ann Luthy, Celestin Webb, Craig Simmons, Debbie McEwen, Edyn Johnson, Evie Shelley, Janell Watson, Jenny Damarjian, Jon Fruehan, Joyce Ostler, Kathy Mallory, Kris Cherrington, Kristi Stewart, Kristina Shelley, Leann Shelley, Leanne Newman, Lisa Jamison, Natalie Bryant, Nola Campbell, Rhonda Fruehan, Ronya Simmons, Scott Jamison, Wanda Wood

In my first book, *Confessions of a Molly Mormon*, I did not name the Eschler Editing team in my acknowledgments, only because I felt concerned that my book did not adequately represent the lofty quality of their services. In that book I chose to violate a number of grammar and punctuation rules since I wanted to create a less formal feeling. Although I have made similar choices in this book, I would be hugely remiss if I did not acknowledge several editors on the Eschler Team who have reviewed and improved my manuscript. From the moment I put it in the capable hands of Angela Eschler herself almost ten years ago, it began to improve. Emily Halverson's early efforts proved to be invaluable. She is the one who sent me on the happy detour that brought *Confessions of a Molly Mormon* into being. Over the last few years Heidi Brockbank has patiently provided her services and has also coordinated the services of others to match my erratic timeline. Most recently Heidi assigned the lovely Lindsay Flanagan to help me with the final edit and other finishing touches. It has been a pleasure and a blessing to work with her and with the entire Eschler Editing team.

And, as in my first book, I again acknowledge my indebtedness to God, who has been at the helm through all my storms even when I didn't know it. He has been my strength and my joy. This book is my gift to Him, an expression of my deep love and gratitude for allowing me to know Him better and to hear and understand His unspoken messages during critical times in my life. My soul praises Him endlessly for His goodness and mercy.

# INTRODUCTION

Like most small children, I must have begun life's journey with an amazing self-image. As a toddler I would climb out of the bathtub, gleefully pat my chubby little thighs, and delightedly chant, "I fatty! I fatty!" My sunny, two-year-old perspective was joyfully untainted and completely self-accepting.

But time marches on, and even in the best of circumstances clouds inevitably cross our paths, weaving shadows into the glorious rays of innocent sunshine. Those shadows can increasingly obscure our vision until we eventually lose sight of who we are. I'm not sure exactly when I first became vulnerable to the influence of those shadows, but at a young age I began chasing the enticing promises of perfectionism, and my life soon became entangled in guilt, fear, anxiety, and shame.

By the time I reached my eighteenth birthday, my self-image had suffered a devastating transformation. On that landmark day I again stood in the bathroom, but this time I was retching over the toilet, secretly trying to throw up every morsel of birthday cake I had just eaten. Though driven by the obsession to acquire a perfectly "skinny" body, I didn't know exactly how skinny I needed to be. All I knew was that I wasn't skinny *enough*. My life was consumed by the urge to hasten toward that nebulous goal because I was convinced that when I reached it, my problems would disappear and I would have everything I wanted.

For seven agonizing years, I lived with my head literally in the toilet. Since eating disorders hadn't yet become a topic of public discussion, I knew of no label for the compulsive behavior that had taken over my life. What I did know was the despair of constant failure as I desperately struggled to escape the grasp of this seemingly invincible monster.

By the time words like anorexia, bulimia, bingeing, and purging had become common in the media, I had been free of my eating disorder for over a decade. My body had stabilized at a comfortable weight and I was the mother of six young children. Unfortunately, the happy life I was seeking still eluded me. Oblivious of the real pathway to happiness, the shadowy illusions of perfectionism continued to rule my world, stealing much of the joy from my parenting and my marriage.

Through the years our children enriched my life beyond measure and we shared many happy times together, but my hunger for an enduring sense of peace and happiness remained unsatisfied. My conflict mostly stemmed from the fear that I wasn't good enough, that my family wasn't good enough, and that we would never be able to measure up to what I felt were God's demands for perfection.

I held the belief—although I would never have admitted it—that if I could somehow make myself good enough, I would be able to control myself, my family, and even the circumstances of our lives so that everything would "turn out right." Only then would I be able to experience the happiness I craved.

Eventually, a huge, menacing cloud covered my path, hovering ominously above me until every tiny ray of sunshine disappeared. Overwhelmed by its shadow, I gave up all hope of ever being happy. During that bleak period, I wished God would let me die and end my miserable journey. Instead, He taught me how to see His divine light shining through the threatening clouds and manage the perfectionism which had dominated my life for far too long. He helped me receive the simple yet powerful gifts that would heal my heart and lead me to a joyful life—the kind of life He desires for all His children.

When I look back on my journey, I sincerely rejoice even though my wanderings took me through dark and difficult terrain. Unexpected twists and turns challenged the very core of my being, but they ultimately led me to a beautiful new understanding of God. He truly does want His children to have joy in this life. Indeed, He wants us to have joy in this very moment! This knowledge has repeatedly lifted me above the clouds of fear and perfectionism, and has granted me many magnificent vistas of understanding and self-acceptance. It's opened my eyes to God's amazing love, and it has allowed me to experience and share that love over and over again.

While the specific details of my journey are uniquely mine, I find many common threads winding throughout my story and the stories of others. Feelings of guilt, shame, insecurity, inferiority, and inadequacy plague men and women alike as we struggle to measure up to artificial, unattainable standards of perfection. We often seek to soothe our pain in destructive or ineffective ways before we discover how to embrace life and receive the joy God intends for us. My journey is a reminder that God's love remains constant throughout the ups and downs of our lives, and that each of our experiences can be turned to our good as we learn to open our hearts to Him.

# 1

# MOSTLY SUNNY WITH A FEW AFTERNOON SHOWERS

*Seeds of perfectionism scattered into my early childhood*

Pleasant memories flood my mind when I reflect on my childhood in rural Idaho. I can still hear my father's clear bass voice as he playfully bounced us on his knee, singing songs from his own childhood about a friendly cow, a foolish old hen, and a trotting little pony. My sister and I giggled in delight as we clung to the wide suspenders of his heavy denim overalls. Daddy's regular chores had all been done and it was too dark to do any more work outside, so it was finally time to settle in for supper.

Music spilled from Daddy's lips like water from a sparkling mountain spring. He must have had more than fifty songs in his ready repertoire, blending melodies of familiar farm animals with tales of ships, trains, and famous or eccentric people. Mother added snippets of harmony as she bustled around the kitchen mashing potatoes, washing the milk bucket, and pouring gravy into a deep Pyrex bowl.

Dishes clattered as my older sister set the table with mismatched plates and silverware. When everything was ready, someone was sent to tell Grandpa it was time to eat. My mother's dad had lived with us for as long as I could remember, and he definitely added his own unique dimension to our family life.

After kneeling for prayer, bodies collided as we eagerly crowded around our small pedestal table. The meal was simple, but food was plentiful. Along with the mounds of mashed potatoes and gravy, we always had carrots from the cellar, home-canned green beans, dense whole wheat bread, freshly churned butter, and delicious raspberry jam. All this was followed by two jars of home-canned peaches or pears for dessert.

While we ate, Mother and Daddy would discuss a fence that needed to be repaired, or the rising price of hay, or the falling price of potatoes, or whatever else had been on their minds that day. As the meal came to an end, Grandpa often posed a riddle. If no one came up with the answer, he would smile slyly and stand to deliver his punch line, punctuating it with a loud slap on the table. We could hear him chuckling all the way down the hall as he returned to his bedroom dragging his left leg slightly, a reminder of a long-ago injury.

Suppertime was often followed by a rousing game of tag. Playful squeals filled the house as we chased each other through the kitchen, down the hall, and back into the living room. When Mother insisted it was time for bed, we reluctantly changed into our pajamas, kissed Daddy goodnight, and promised we'd wake up smiling for him—a ritual which began when he said all he wanted for his birthday was happy, smiling children.

After saying my personal prayers, I would snuggle into bed to the whisper of the wind in the cottonwood trees and the rush of irrigation water tumbling over the little waterfall at the end of our lane. Most often I could hear the muffled tones of Mother's voice reading to Daddy as they lay next to each other in the adjoining room, their occasional bursts of hushed laughter floating to my ears as I drifted off to sleep.

Other lovely scenes fill my mind when I revisit those early years with my family. I see us lying on the lawn at night, gazing up in wonder at a sky crammed full of brilliant stars, searching for our favorite constellations. I see us roasting hot dogs and marshmallows over the coals of a waning bonfire. I see a row of shivering bodies spread across our cement patio trying to soak in the sun's warmth after playing in the frigid irrigation water. The life my parents provided for us still seems like an ideal way to raise a child.

As of Jesus Christ of Latter-day Saints, religion permeated our family life. We always said a blessing on the food before each meal, knelt for family prayer every night, and attended church meetings both morning and evening on Sundays. We paid tithing and made other monetary donations regularly in spite of our tight finances. Although Primary disrupted their work day and also required a weekly monetary investment for gas, my parents considered this religious training a necessity for their children.

In church meetings, I learned that our goal was to become perfect like Heavenly Father and Jesus and that if our whole family could possibly manage to become perfect, we would earn the reward of being allowed to live together forever in the highest part of heaven called the Celestial Kingdom. Undoubtedly my teachers intended this doctrine to be comforting to me, but what I took from it was that I had to be perfect and make it to the Celestial Kingdom or I would be forever separated from my family. That was an unbearable thought to me.

Even as a young child, though, I quickly realized that no matter how hard I tried, I couldn't make myself be good all the time. Every single night I prayed that God would "make me a good little girl" but the very next day I would turn around and do something I knew I shouldn't. Sometimes I lied to my mother to avoid being spanked. Other times I said or did mean things to my siblings. I didn't like sharing, and when treats were passed around I always wanted the biggest one. Though I knew I was being "bad," I couldn't seem to help myself. How was I ever going to make myself perfect so God would let me be with my family forever?

My father was the best person I knew, and I absolutely adored him. In my mind, he was definitely going to the Celestial Kingdom. He was a patient, hard-working man who loved his wife, his children, his farm, and his neighbors. He saw goodness in everyone. I knew he loved God because of the tender way he handled his black leather-bound scriptures each time he took them down from the top shelf in the living room. We weren't allowed to touch those two special books, but I liked to sit beside him on the couch and look at the tiny words covering the delicate pages.

Daddy reminded us to kneel and say our personal prayers before jumping into bed at night, and he constantly encouraged us to be "peacemakers." Always soft-spoken, his preferred method of discipline was a few minutes sitting on a chair. I felt wonderfully secure in his love, and I tried hard not to disappoint him.

My relationship with my mother was much more complicated. She was every bit as essential to my sense of security as my father was, but I never would have said I adored her. As a no-nonsense disciplinarian, she expected us to do *as* we were told, *when* we were told. A disobedient child often received several swats to the backside with a wooden spatula. As a result, I generally felt somewhat afraid of my mother. Her fiery spirit was the driving force in our home, and we all tried to avoid upsetting her.

But Mother wasn't all harshness. She often sang as she worked and she loved telling stories of her childhood "back home" in Australia. When she assigned us long, monotonous tasks such as weeding the carrots or picking the raspberries, she worked along with us as often as she could. She tried to make the job as pleasant as possible by teaching us fun new songs or challenging our minds with math problems. She had a deep appreciation for nature and would happily pause to point out an unusual cloud formation, a mouse nest she had uncovered, or a crane that caught her eye as it skimmed along the bank of the river.

Mother was capable and creative. As a seamstress, she had few equals, and her gardening and veterinary skills were admired throughout the valley. She could wield a hammer as well as any man and did much of the construction and finishing work on our home. Whenever a task needed to be done, she often already knew "the best way" to do it. If she didn't, she would seek out a teacher or a book of instructions and would soon have mastered yet another skill.

The only thing Mother couldn't seem to master was her weight. Year after year we listened to her mournful refrain, "I'd be happy if I could just lose thirty pounds!" The number of pounds changed from time to time, but her intense desire to lose weight never changed. When she dieted, she often skipped supper or ate at the counter so she wouldn't be tempted by the "fattening foods" the rest of us were having. But suppertime felt incomplete when Mother didn't sit down with us, and I was always glad when she ended her diet and joined us again at the table.

Undoubtedly Mother's passionate desire to be thinner contributed to my later obsession with my own weight, but it would be a mistake to say that she was responsible for my eating disorder. My perfectionistic thinking would have certainly manifested itself regardless. Throughout my struggle, Mother yearned for my happiness and did her best to help and support me even though I never shared specific details of my battle with her.

During my earliest years, my favorite playmate was my brother, Gaven. We had a sister who was several years older, but Gaven was born just a year before I was, and I quickly claimed him as my best buddy. I followed him everywhere. We waded through irrigation ditches, wandered among the cottonwood trees searching for bird nests, ran through the corral with baby lambs trailing at our heels, and pushed each other on our big tire swing. He was my hero because he came up with so many fun things to do, and because he dared to do scary things like climbing tall trees and jumping into the pig pen.

A few years later, my younger sister, Janell, began playing a significant role in my life as well. She came to the family two years after I did, and would eventually share my bedroom, my chores, and many of my secrets. She was barely a toddler when she began to tag along with Gaven and me on our wonderful adventures.

At first, I didn't mind having Janell join us. Since I was the big sister she usually did whatever I told her to do. However, there came a time when Gaven began taking Janell on his adventures without asking me to come with them. They would sneak off before I even knew they were going. I felt hurt and confused.

I wanted to reclaim my preferred status with Gaven, but the harder I tried, the greater the distance between us grew. We still played tag together and did other fun activities as a family, but my best buddy had clearly replaced me. Feelings of rejection and jealousy popped up regularly.

Because I was a very social child, I sought out friends at church to ease my sense of loneliness, and I jumped at every opportunity to be away from home. I liked Wednesdays because I got to go to Primary, but my favorite day of the week was Sunday. On Sundays, Mother would let me go home with a friend after morning church, and we would have five or six hours to play together before returning for the evening meeting. During those wonderful hours, I once again had a friend who belonged only to me. I didn't have to compete for their attention.

Another thing that seemed to soothe the pain of rejection was praise, glorious praise! I thrived on it. Praise felt amazing, especially when I was praised for being *better* than someone else. For example, my dad praised me for putting away my coat and boots when my siblings didn't, my Primary teacher praised me for being quiet when others were noisy, my mother praised me for helping with the dishes when my siblings slipped outside to play. I didn't always *want* to do praiseworthy things, but I craved the praise. I desperately wanted to be especially "good" all the time so I could keep a steady flow of praise coming my way.

While most children enjoy being praised, children who deal with perfectionism tend to go to extremes. They often develop a compelling drive to please and impress *everyone*. They measure their worth by the praise they receive. They push themselves obsessively to be better than those around them, always afraid of losing the favor they have gained. As one of these children, the shadows of perfectionism began sucking the joy out of my young life even though I had no idea they existed.

# 2

# HEAVY CLOUDS ROLL IN

*Guilt and shame grow in my early years;*
*a sexual abuse experience*

My world expanded immensely when I started elementary school. Since I liked being around people, and especially kids my own age, I was thrilled by the increased opportunity to socialize. I enjoyed the routine of school, and I loved learning new things. I memorized quickly and thrived on my teacher's praise. Her bold red 100 at the top of my completed assignments meant everything to me.

Most people want to be noticed and feel important. Perhaps perfectionists feel that desire more keenly than others because they so often judge themselves to be less adequate than those around them. During first grade, I felt important because I almost always occupied the first chair in the top reading group. My self-worth was reaffirmed every morning as the teacher called out the names of those she deemed worthy of being in that group. Day after day, my name was called first, which meant I got to sit at the head of the circle. When everyone was seated, the teacher called on us in random order to read aloud. Each day I kept my position in the circle by reading flawlessly.

Then one day, tragedy struck. It was my first day back after having missed several days of school, and when I opened my book I saw something on the page that was alarmingly unfamiliar. It was a simple hyphenated word, but my whole body broke into a sweat, and my decoding skills flew right out the window. In desperation, I turned to a classmate for help, but the teacher's eagle eye was on us, enforcing her strict no-talking rule.

As usual, she called me to the first chair, and after everyone else had taken their places in the circle, we began to read. I hoped and prayed someone else would be assigned to tackle that mysterious word before the teacher called on me, but it was not to be. I started reading with a confidence I didn't feel, and when I came to that strange word, rather than admit I didn't know how to say it, I made a pathetic little grunt and hurried on. Of course, the teacher stopped me, and with an amused little smile, she asked me to repeat what I had just said.

Tears sprang to my eyes and I silently stared at the blurring words. My face and ears burned bright red. After a long pause, my teacher asked in her demeaning teacher voice if anyone in the circle would like to "help" me. I'd heard that tone in her words before, but never in reference to me. Feelings of shame flooded over me as eager hands shot up to volunteer their superior knowledge. Here was a chance to advance to that coveted first chair.

I knew the drill. As soon as the correct pronunciation was given I reluctantly stood up to await my verdict. Usually, the teacher directed one or two children to move up, thereby rearranging the order only slightly, but this time she had every single child in the group advance, leaving me to occupy the very last chair. As I sat down in complete disgrace, my sense of self-worth vanished, taking with it every trace of my fragile happiness.

Throughout the rest of the week, I feverishly practiced the reading assignments, and on Friday my name was again the first one called. Though I felt triumphant as I took my place at the head of the circle again, that experience left a deep scar. For the rest of the school year, and for many school years thereafter, I felt a sense of underlying stress every day, worrying and wondering if my preparation had been sufficient to prevent another devastating moment of humiliation.

Upon entering second grade, my waning self-confidence was dealt another huge blow when I discovered that Kathy, a new girl in our class, could read almost as well as the teacher. Astonished that anyone my age could be so smart, I felt desperately lost as I struggled to find some other meaningful identity. I had no idea I could be happy being anything less than the best. My motivation to work hard in school diminished because I obviously couldn't catch up with Kathy's reading skills, let alone become better than she was. It seemed useless to try when I was clearly facing the impossible.

To make matters worse, one day when our teacher announced that it was time for our weekly square-dance class, Jim, the boy who had always chosen me for his dance partner, chose Kathy instead. For as long as I could remember, I had felt a special claim on Jim. We had played together since we were babies because our mothers were best friends. Jim had been my security blanket when we started school, always including me in playground games and choosing me as his dance partner. I had tried to dismiss some recent little changes in his behavior, but now the truth was undeniable before me, and I was powerless to do anything about it. Not only was I left unhappily partnered with my short little cousin, but I was once more left with a sense of deep loss.

My dwindling self-esteem took a devastating hit the following year by an incident of my own creation. One wintry day, not wanting to face the cold temperatures outside or the rejection I so often felt on the playground, I devised a plan to give myself a reprieve from both. I carefully composed a note telling my teacher that I should be excused from going out to recess. I signed my mother's name, assuming my teacher would never know since I had now learned to write in *cursive* just like adults did.

I was delighted when recess time came and the teacher sent everyone outside to play except for me. However, I felt anything but delighted when she walked down the aisle and placed the offending note in front of me. After a long pause, she told me I should be ashamed of myself, and that I had been foolish to think she wouldn't recognize my handwriting. Then she stated and restated how disappointed my parents were going to be when they found out what I had done.

After what felt like an eternity, she ended her lecture and sent me outside. For the rest of the recess, I stood next to the cold brick wall of the old school house, shivering and alone, watching my classmates play hopscotch, jump rope, and dodgeball.

When the bell rang and the class was seated, instead of starting our regular lessons, the teacher stood and held up the note I had written. She explained in detail what I had done and warned everyone not to try anything so foolish. I fought tears of anger and humiliation as all eyes turned on me, some sneaking sideways glances, others blatantly staring. The previous year I had lost my prominent place as the best reader, and now I had totally disgraced myself by trying to deceive the teacher so I could stay in during recess.

Throughout the rest of the day, I wallowed in self-pity, but by the next morning I had a new plan. When I got out of bed, I coughed and complained, doing everything I could think of to convince my mother I was sick. She was skeptical, but I gave it my best effort and she finally agreed to let me stay home. I was thrilled.

After the bus picked up my siblings, however, I wasn't clever enough to continue my act. The immediate change in my behavior confirmed what Mother had already suspected. I can still see her sitting in the rocking chair nursing my baby sister as she began the interrogation. Her probing questions didn't let up until I burst into tears and confessed that I was too embarrassed to face my teacher and classmates because I had told a lie.

At that point I fully expected the wooden spatula to come rattling out of the utensil drawer. After all, Mother had always said she would spank us harder for telling a lie than for disobeying. But this time there was no spatula. Instead, Mother reached out and gently gathered me to her side, holding me close as my tears trailed shame and sorrow down my cheeks and onto my nightgown.

I was too young to understand how deeply my mother must have felt my pain, but when she spoke, her voice was unusually tender. She talked about how miserable life can be when you tell one lie to cover another because then there has to be another lie and then another and another, until you can't keep all the lies straight in your own head. My eight-year-old mind didn't grasp the wisdom of her words, but I understood one thing for sure: this kind of humiliation had to be avoided at all costs. I must try harder to be good, and when I failed, I had to be better at concealing it.

Once Janell started school she quickly caught up with me in every subject. She had a sharp mind and she loved to read. Shadows of jealousy, competition, and inferiority crossed my path with increasing frequency. I didn't compete with my older sister who was four years ahead of me or with my brother who didn't care about school, but Janell was always right at my heels. On the one hand, I admired her abilities, but on the other hand, I was threatened by the fact that she was my academic equal even though she was two grades behind me.

More feelings of inferiority crept in at our annual family reunions. I loved playing with my cousins, but I noticed that the families who lived in the city had newer cars, wore cuter clothing, and lived in nicer houses than we did. Some of them even got to take singing and dancing lessons, which seemed much more impressive and exciting than my boring piano lessons.

In all my comparing, however, I did find myself feeling superior to people who didn't dress as well as we did or who lived in dilapidated old houses. Most of those families had rattle-trap cars that broke down regularly, so the kids couldn't always get to church. Some of their parents even smoked and drank. Although my clothes weren't fashionable, they were washed and well-kept, and although we didn't own a fancy home, ours was clean, organized, and welcoming. Surely we were better than those people!

Comparing has a way of nurturing seeds of judgment, jealousy, and envy. The more I focused on what people owned and how they dressed, the more I longed to have nicer things. I often valued my relationships with people according to their possessions. Of course, I didn't realize it at the time, but I was continually fueling the belief that having more than others made me better than they were, and that being better than others would make me happy.

Though I was carefully taught that expensive possessions tend to make people proud and therefore less pleasing to God, that didn't stop me from wanting what others had. It just made me feel guilty. In my church classes I gave all the right answers about sharing and loving and not allowing jealousy to rule our lives, but secretly, I could see the gap growing between my true feelings and the perfection I was aspiring to attain.

My greatest fear of God's rejection stemmed from my sexual curiosity. Early scoldings had taught me it was "nasty" to touch certain parts of my body, but that had done nothing to curb my curiosity and its associated pleasures. No matter what anyone said, I was frequently drawn in that direction. It was my deep, dark, little-girl secret. Then, when I was about six or seven, a solitary incident occurred that greatly intensified my sexual focus and guilt.

It was a lazy summer day and some relatives had dropped by for an afternoon visit. They rarely came to our house, so my parents happily invited them on a tour of our beautiful vegetable and flower gardens. The wife eagerly accepted, but the husband declined the invitation saying he was tired and preferred to stay out of the sun. He sat down and settled into an overstuffed chair in our living room.

I don't remember how I came to be alone with this man, but he briefly engaged me in conversation and then asked me if I would like some candy from his car. I hadn't been around him much before, and I wasn't really comfortable with him, but I loved candy and I generally trusted adults, so I eagerly followed him outside. When he opened the car door, I expected him to reach inside for the candy, but instead, he got into the car, lifted me onto his lap, and closed the door behind us. My uneasy feelings gave way to disappointment when he handed me a cheap little penny sucker. I had hoped for so much more.

Suddenly I was stunned by inappropriate touching. Sparing the details, I will simply say it sent fireworks through my young body that should never have been his privilege to ignite. He kept saying I was a good little girl and promised to bring me a lot more candy the next time he came. Finally, after telling me I should keep this "our own little secret," he opened the door, set me on the ground, and sent me back to the house.

When I was young, sexual topics were taboo, so sexual abuse and how to deal with it weren't openly discussed like they are today. But even if I had been taught, I'm not sure I would have chosen to tell anyone. The experience felt too shocking, too wrong, too personal to share. It triggered a mountain of confusion, guilt, and shame. I had no words to explain my mixed up feelings— just vivid memories replaying in my mind of the man's voice, the smell of his breath, the disappointing candy, the sounds, and the sensation I experienced. Besides, I felt certain my parents would be upset and I didn't want to be a problem. Without question, this had to be "my own little secret."

And over the next few years, I carefully guarded another secret—the secret that I occasionally agreed to be the "patient" for my bolder girlfriends who liked to play "doctor." If the risk of getting caught seemed small, I was usually willing. The guilt I felt may have reduced the number of occurrences, but it certainly didn't reduce my fascination with my sexuality.

For myself and my friends, our sexual interest and experiences were definitely in conflict with the concepts of purity we were being taught. To my knowledge, most of these young girls had isolated experiences comparable to mine, although I know that one eight-year-old was dealing with ongoing abuse from a teenage uncle.

From an adult perspective, it's easy to see that everyone must face their own sexuality at some point. When and how that happens is obviously going to vary, depending on the person, how they are taught, and how they interpret their personal experiences. Teaching sexual purity is a tricky business. Saying that all things sexual are sacred and should be saved for marriage sounds simple enough until you consider how it leaves children and young people feeling when their experiences don't fall within those boundaries.

As I have shared my experiences with others, people have sometimes opened up about their own experiences. Through our conversations, I have come to realize that many children experience something related to their sexuality that is disturbing to them. It may be caused by abuse, by their own experimentation, by media exposure, or by a combination of these things. Depending on how they internalize what they are taught, their experiences can easily lead to inappropriate guilt and shame, and to acting out in self-destructive ways. They can also make it more difficult to create a healthy intimate relationship in marriage.

Therapists and researchers have concluded that sexual abuse often contributes to eating disorders, perfectionism, anxiety, and a host of other emotion-based behavioral challenges. While there is no way to know just how much one specific incident impacted my later choices, my sexual curiosity and experiences certainly filled my heart with guilt and shame from an early age. These feelings easily intertwined with all my other fears and insecurities to create a recurring storm. I sought to shelter myself from that storm by finding ways to win more praise and approval.

When I could no longer derive my sense of self-worth from my academic superiority, I found a measure of comfort in the praise I received for my perfect church attendance, and for my model behavior in Sunday School and Primary. My teachers' compliments, along with their glowing reports to my parents, pushed me to be even more impressive. I always listened attentively to the stories my teachers told and did my best to remember every detail so I could be the clever one with all the right answers.

Stories about Jesus instantaneously healing sick people amazed me, and I especially loved to hear how He brought a little girl back to life after she had already died. Most of the time, though, my mind returned to stories about God punishing people. I thought of the time He had an angel destroy all the firstborn Egyptians, and then their army was swallowed up in the Red Sea because they didn't want to let Moses and his people leave. I thought of all the people who were drowned in the flood because they didn't repent even though Noah had warned them. I imagined children who were just as terrified of death as I was, scrambling to the very top of a high mountain trying desperately to escape the rising water.

Because of my frequent desire to be selfish or disobedient, pondering these stories created deep anxiety in my soul. I assumed I belonged to that group of people who deserved God's punishment. I didn't know when or how He might decide to punish me, but I was certain I wasn't good enough for Him. Surely I was doomed if I didn't somehow get my act together. But how could I possibly make myself perfect so I could be safe from His angry judgments?

When I was a little older, I learned about a huge fire that was supposed to be coming in the last days to cleanse the earth of all wickedness. I wasn't clear on the details, but the way I understood the story, there would be two girls standing together in a field. One girl would be consumed by the fire because she had been wicked, but the other would remain untouched. Not even the hem of her robe would be scorched because she had earned God's protection by always being good. (See Matthew 24:40–41)

My anxious little mind repeatedly imagined Janell and me standing near our house, gazing awestruck at a wall of flames rushing toward us across our west field. I saw myself frozen in terror as the fire swept over us. Then I saw my sister standing there all by herself, untouched by the fire, looking all around, wondering where I had gone. But no trace of my body remained. Not even ashes. I had completely vanished because I wasn't good enough for God.

My fears and budding perfectionism so completely dominated my thinking that there was no room in my heart for the truth of God's merciful, loving nature. Although I continued to pray every night asking Him to "make me a good little girl," I didn't believe He had any desire to help me become that good little girl. I viewed Him as an angry judge just watching and waiting—waiting to see if I could somehow pull off perfection. And the coming storms were only going to strengthen my fearful thinking.

# 3

# STORMY WITH
# INTERMITTENT SUNSHINE

*Seeking self-worth; another sexual abuse experience*

By the end of third grade, my self-image had been completely altered. I felt totally insignificant, although I often fantasized about being someone special—someone smarter than Kathy, someone prettier than Jeanne, someone more artistic than Mary, someone who could play the piano even better than Cindy. I thought I would be happy if I could just be someone else—someone wonderfully talented who actually deserved the constant praise and admiration I desired.

In my search for self-worth, I found some satisfaction in being identified at home as the most orderly child in the family. With ten of us in the household, things often got chaotic, especially when Mother worked outside, which she often did. Daddy craved order, and he abundantly praised my efforts to keep the house clean. He supported me when I complained about things left lying around, or about someone messing up the kitchen after I had just cleaned it.

I took great pride in keeping my side of the bedroom clean and made sure it always compared favorably to the way Janell's side looked. I loved the feeling of control my tidiness gave me. I also liked feeling superior in at least one way to this little sister whose academic brilliance threatened me. In all actuality, Janell was my dearest friend, and I would have been totally lost without her. Still, my growing perfectionism threw subtle wedges into our relationship—and probably into all my relationships—even though I didn't understand what was happening.

My quest to feel better about myself persisted, but for a few years, I seemed to be stuck with little opportunity to improve my self-image. However, once I turned twelve, the weekly Saturday night dances at the church provided new opportunities for me to socialize and seek approval. Our family was always among the first to arrive and the last to leave since my parents were the dance directors. They unlocked the closet which guarded the old record player, selected the music from tall stacks of vinyl records, and then locked everything up again at midnight when the dance ended.

I loved the music, the socializing, and the privilege of staying out late. About the time I started going to the dances, a new boy in my sixth-grade class started coming with his older sister. He danced almost exclusively with me, and after a while, he started calling me ahead of time to make sure I was planning to meet him at the dance. I felt special because I didn't have to sit among the cluster of "wallflowers" hoping that someone besides my dad or my brother would ask me to dance.

While my social world was expanding in this delightful new way, an experience with my older sister's former boyfriend dramatically expanded my sense of guilt and shame. Even though my sister no longer dated this boy, our family continued to welcome him into our hearts and our home. He had joined the military after high school and was stationed at a base just a few hours away, so he came for overnight visits whenever he was on leave. I felt flattered when he told us he preferred to spend his free time with us on the farm rather than with his own family.

One day I was in the basement playing ping pong with him when he offered to give me a back rub. I'd never had a massage before and his offer made me uncomfortable. I told him I just wanted to play ping pong, but he kept coaxing me, insisting he knew I would love it. The situation got more and more awkward, and, being a pleaser, I was afraid of hurting his feelings or making him upset. Since he wasn't taking no for an answer, I finally gave in and followed his directions to lie face down on the couch.

As his hands moved rhythmically across my shoulders and down my spine, I was unimpressed. "So, what's the big deal?" I thought. "I'd much rather be playing ping pong." But soon his hands slipped under my shirt and then around to my chest. Once again, a man's hands were unexpectedly igniting those fireworks.

My head felt like it was going to explode. A million conflicting voices screamed at me through the silence. What was happening was unquestionably wrong and I knew I should get the heck out of there, but it did feel *enjoyable*—however shamefully so—and the damage was already done. I had already let it go too far. What could I do now? How would he react if I tried to stop him? What could I possibly say that wouldn't be horribly embarrassing for both of us? What if he got mad? I feared that my mother and sisters would be upset with me if I got him in trouble and he decided not to come back again.

My frantic mind concluded that I should pretend to fall asleep and hope he would go away. Though my brain was on high alert, I forced myself to breathe slowly, loudly and deliberately. Finally, I heard his footsteps going up the wooden stairs.

Suddenly I wanted to scream or bang my head on the cinderblock wall—anything to stop myself from thinking and feeling. How would I ever handle this overwhelming guilt? All I knew was that I couldn't tell anyone. I didn't want to get in trouble, and I didn't want anyone to know how pathetically weak I was. Everyone would be so disappointed in me, and any glorious praise would be replaced with disdain. Worst of all, there was no way I could plead innocent because I hadn't chosen to leave, even after I realized serious trouble was afoot.

Anguish consumed me. I felt absolutely driven to do *something*, but what was there for me to do? Eventually, I calmed my mind enough to compose a carefully worded note. I said that I thought we should "nip this in the bud," but that I hoped we could still be friends. Because I didn't have the courage to face him, I put the note in an envelope and stealthily slipped it into the pocket of his coat where it hung in the living room closet.

The next time this young man returned to our home, he totally avoided me. He played games with my little sisters and helped them with their chores, but he deliberately excluded me whenever I tried to join them. I felt deeply hurt and resentful, but I never said a word to anyone. Really, what was there for me to say, and who would I say it to? We both knew he was in complete control. He continued to come periodically until he was transferred overseas and our family lost contact with him.

It's maddening to consider how much control a perpetrator can exercise over his victims by taking advantage of their desire to be accepted, by preying on their feelings of guilt and shame, or by threatening their loved ones. Though the seriousness of my experience is trivial compared to what millions of other women and children suffer, it still left an indelible mark on my life. I stuffed my secret deep inside where it constantly festered and resurfaced, reminding me that I was unworthy of anyone's praise or respect and totally unworthy of God's acceptance or affection.

Fifteen years later, I found out I wasn't the only one in my family affected by this young man's sexual obsession. My little sister had started going to counseling for severe depression, and in one of her sessions, she finally revealed the nightmare this young man had inflicted on her. He had violated her repeatedly over the course of his many visits and had secured her silence by threatening to kill our parents if she told anyone.

When I heard her story, I became physically ill. I realized that if I hadn't been so worried about protecting myself, she might have been spared some, if not all, of his abuse. Fortunately, over time, and with the help of further counseling, my sister has been able to release the pain of those experiences and leave this man in God's hands. We have shared our story from time to time encouraging others, both victims and predators, to seek help and healing.

Even though sexual memories, curiosity, and feelings continued to cast haunting shadows across my path, we humans are amazingly resilient, and the next few years proved to be a relatively happy season of my life. Besides my little Saturday-night-dance romance, I belonged to our church softball team and attended early morning practices with my sister. The older girls inspired me to work hard and they celebrated every improvement, generously feeding my hunger for praise.

An even more significant reason for this happier season was a remarkable seventh-grade teacher who reawakened my desire to excel academically. In contrast to the more matronly teachers at our school, Anna McHenry was a classy, professional woman. She spoke with an endearing lisp, and her energy and enthusiasm were contagious. She was attentive to everyone and saw only greatness in her students.

Mrs. McHenry filled the classroom with maps of faraway places and required us to study current events, opening our minds to the world beyond our sheltered little valley. Her optimistic expectations proved to be an academic turning point for many of her students, and especially for me. By the end of the following year, I ranked third in our eighth-grade graduating class. It felt good to be back in the academic limelight, but of course, I secretly coveted the positions of the two students who ranked ahead of me.

# 4

# A NEW STORM SYSTEM
# MOVES IN

*I need a perfect body!*

The innocent romance that had begun at the Saturday night dances flourished for almost two years. Even though I didn't think my boyfriend was the coolest guy around, I still felt special because he chose me over all the other girls. I envied those who captured the attention of the more popular guys, but I felt superior to those who had no boyfriend at all.

Eventually, my fragile security was shaken when my boyfriend's interest drifted elsewhere. I didn't exactly miss him, but I missed feeling special. I missed knowing that someone would be waiting for me each week when I arrived at the dance. Although I still looked forward to the dances, I was back to worrying about being stuck on the sidelines with a phony smile plastered on my face, praying that some cute guy would ask me to dance.

Soon I found a new boyfriend, but again he wasn't from the cool crowd. He was two years older than me and significantly more experienced than my earlier boyfriend. He was good at engaging hormones, but he didn't push for more than kissing. I loved his attention and the magic of feeling desired.

Pursuing my dream of a social break-through, I involved myself in as many school clubs and activities as my parents would allow. I made new friends, held leadership positions, and received a variety of awards, but nothing made me feel happy and secure for long. I envied those funny, quick-witted students who drew others to them so effortlessly. Even though I wasn't comfortable when I interacted with most of the kids in the popular crowd, I still longed to be a part of their circle.

High school provided more opportunities for dating, but I had no success attracting the guys I really wanted to go out with. As I endlessly mulled over my situation, I realized the cheerleaders and other girls who commanded the popular boys' attention were not only fun and witty, they were generally petite and slender. I quickly succumbed to the recurring thought that my weight was the root of my problem.

Perhaps that conclusion was influenced by my mother's endless battle with her weight, or by frequent conversations with friends about tiny waistlines and perfect hourglass figures. It was definitely perpetuated by the chart our P.E. teacher hung in the locker room. She posted it next to the door by the scale and told us to see where we fell between underweight and morbidly obese. Comparing weight became a part of the class routine, especially among the popular crowd. I listened attentively for the numbers when other girls were asked how much they weighed, but I hated being asked to reveal my own weight.

Once I identified my weight as my fundamental problem, I promised myself I would quickly lose those ugly extra pounds that made my waist too thick and my thighs so flabby. I tried jogging, but I found it both painful and boring. Restricting my food intake seemed to be a more viable tactic for me, and I knew exactly where to go for dieting advice. My mother happily shared her ideas and enthusiastically supported my efforts as I set goals and counted calories just as she did.

Because I so desperately wanted to be popular and skinny, I became distraught when I found it nearly impossible to stick with my diet. I berated myself angrily whenever I gave in to "fattening" temptations. Mother was eager for me to succeed where she had failed, but I didn't appreciate her monitoring my portions or telling me I shouldn't eat something I was about to put in my mouth.

When I managed to eat sparingly for several days, I would notice my stomach was a little flatter and my weight had dropped slightly. Standing in front of the mirror I would ecstatically turn from side to side, visualizing how much better I was going to look once I lost even more. I would happily tell myself I was on my way to being wonderfully skinny and totally desirable to the cutest guys out there. But soon I would lose control and eat much more than I intended to. Those few pounds would return, and I'd plummet into despair and self-disdain. How could I be so weak? Why had I allowed myself to ruin all my progress? I was so stupid! Was I stuck being fat forever? What was the matter with me, anyway?

Despite my perceived weight problem, I had several steady boyfriends during those early high school years. None of them were part of the popular crowd, but for me, almost any boyfriend was better than no boyfriend. One time my brother expressed concern about a guy I was dating because he overheard him talking crudely about girls, but I didn't break up with him because of my overriding need for male attention.

Although I craved the feeling of complete acceptance that came with *making out*—the term we used for passionate hugging and kissing—lessons taught by my church teachers convinced me it was easy to unintentionally "get in trouble." Being pregnant or even indulging in heavy petting was something my carefully guarded reputation couldn't afford, so I established a couple of hard and fast dating rules: no hands in private places, and no French kissing. Other than that, I was generally a willing participant. My letter-of-the-law attitude most assuredly helped me avoid some inappropriate situations, but it did nothing to bridle my passion for physical attention, nor did it increase my ability to receive comfort and guidance from the Spirit.

At the end of each date, my boyfriend would park in front of my house and we would steam up the car windows. For me, it was the high point of the evening. Making out was my "drug of choice." All my insecurities and guilt melted away in the darkness as I drank in the euphoric pleasure of feeling completely desired. During those blissful moments, I finally felt like I was enough. This magical feeling allowed me to temporarily forget all my fears and my guilt, even though I knew deep down it was all a lie—this was not *real* love, and all my insecurities would return with the morning light.

It might be said that I was love-starved, which in fact I was, even though I had a wonderful family that loved and cared for me, and sometimes I even had a boyfriend who declared his undying love. The love I was starving for, however, is the love that has the power to bring lasting self-acceptance and security—that pure, beautiful love which can come only from God. I'm sure I was taught about that kind of love more than once, but I still had deep, shadowy valleys to travel before I would be ready to set aside my insecurities and perfectionism and receive the precious healing influence of God's love.

Meanwhile, I continued to flounder and search among the counterfeits.

One of the boys I dated was bold enough to confront me about my inappropriate behavior. We were on our way home after a movie one night when he turned into the corner of a secluded parking lot. He was dashingly handsome, and at first, his passionate kisses thrilled me, but I became nervous when I found myself repeatedly redirecting his persistent attempts to touch my body beyond my pre-determined boundaries.

Suddenly he brusquely pushed me away. "What's that about?" he demanded.

I felt his eyes peering sharply at me through the darkness, but I made no reply. There was ice in his words when he finally broke the silence, "If you don't want it, don't act like you do." Then the engine roared to life and without another word he sped angrily toward my home.

I felt embarrassed, offended, and falsely accused. But I knew in my heart he was right. I was supposed to be a "good" girl, firmly committed to standards of conduct that would lead to a temple marriage, but in reality, I was using him to get my high. While most of my boyfriends at least shared my religion, this boy wasn't even a member of my church. Though I was wildly attracted to him physically, we shared no common foundation for building a lasting relationship.

It would be nice if I could say I was more circumspect after that experience, but it would be totally untrue. Yes, I felt guilty for setting a poor example. And yes, I wanted to avoid similar situations in the future. But I was not ready to face the truth and cease my frantic pursuit of love and acceptance in all the wrong ways.

Throughout my early high school years I continued to attend the Saturday night dances, but a bizarre routine developed. All week I would look forward to the dance with excited anticipation. The fantasy of being wrapped in Prince Charming's embrace was intoxicating, and I could hardly wait.

But when Saturday morning rolled around, my fears took over. I fretted and stewed about what I could possibly wear to appear skinnier and more alluring. I desperately wanted to avoid being a wallflower. The hours just before the dance were torture as I fussed to get every hair in place and rifled through my wardrobe trying on every possible outfit. Even with the help of a rib-crushing, tummy-tucking corset, nothing ever made me look skinny enough.

Mother's patience stretched thin as she tried to help me regain a more realistic perspective. She constantly assured me I looked great and reminded me that I always enjoyed the dances no matter what I wore. But my anxiety was never appeased. Things could be different this time!

Sometimes Mother went through the ordeal of making a new dress for me, hoping to help me feel better about myself. Even though she easily created beautiful dresses for my sisters, whenever she sewed for me it was an exercise in frustration for both of us. The patterns never matched my disproportionate body shape, so making clothes for me required multiple fittings and substantial alterations.

During one of those dreaded fittings, I stood in front of the mirror taking stock of my figure while Mother sat nearby at the sewing machine. My self-disdain grew as I loudly listed each of my unacceptable features—my big nose, my left ear that stuck out, my uneven shoulders, my wide ribcage, my thick waist, my flabby legs, my lopsided hips. Mother listened in silent dismay until I started criticizing my knees.

At that point, she jumped to her feet, lifted her skirt to expose her own knees, and pointed out emphatically that I was not alone because her knees looked exactly like mine. My quick retort was thoughtless and cruel. "Well then, I guess it's your fault that I have these hideous knees. Why did you give me such an ugly body, anyway?"

I regretted those biting words even before I saw my mother's tears, but there was no way to undo the damage. I hadn't meant to hurt her. I was just venting my own pain. It was devastating to realize that my insensitive words had impacted my commanding, invincible mother enough to make her cry. Mother never cried. Never! Bringing her to tears was conclusive evidence that I was indeed a wicked person. What hope was there that I could ever make myself good enough for God?

Not surprisingly, my mother's attempts to please me with a new dress rarely paid off. Sometimes I would think it made me look fat right from the beginning. Other times I thought I looked okay until I got to the dance and compared myself to the cuter, skinnier girls. Then it became painfully clear that I needed much more than a new dress. I had to have that skinny body!

Pressure on young women to be skinny increased when Twiggy, an English model, became an overnight sensation during the mid-sixties. Women had been dieting for years, but Twiggy was a teenager and she strongly appealed to the younger population. Her name summed up her unnaturally skinny appearance. The healthy Doris Day look of the previous era was out, and Twiggy's wispy look was suddenly the one to copy.

Miniskirts came in with Twiggy, and I became keenly aware of the new trend even though we didn't have a television in our home and we never bought fashion magazines. Twiggy was the talk of teenage girls everywhere, as well as the talk of their mothers. Hem lengths took a sudden leap upward. The generation gap became more pronounced as girls who wanted to be in style clashed with parents who insisted on old-fashioned modesty.

One day while I was at a friend's house, I caught a little snippet of a Twiggy interview. She was asked what girls should do if they hadn't been blessed with good-looking legs. I can still hear her flippant response, punctuated sharply by her crisp British accent. "Well," she said, "I guess the poor little loves had better stay home then!"

A wave of anger and despair swept over me. I was mortified to be one of the "poor little loves" who should "stay home." But my self-worth depended on my social life and there was no way I could stay home, regardless of how ugly I thought my knees were. Even though I desperately wanted to belong to the "in-crowd," the best I could do was continue to cover my hideous knees with longer hemlines and act like I didn't care that I was out of fashion.

Ironically, most people saw my longer skirts as a sign that I was being true to the standards of my religion. Thus, I won further, though undeserved, praise from church leaders and others who saw me as the model young woman. With all my lurking insecurities, this image was challenging to maintain, but I knew what I had to do, and I did my best to play the game. Little did I know that I was on the verge of a whole new game with a whole new set of complicated rules.

# 5

# BRILLIANT SUNSHINE

*The perfect boyfriend and the perfect solution
to my weight problem*

Early in my senior year I went to a school dance with a girl friend. The room was dark and the music was loud. We sat down and I turned toward my friend to hear what she was saying. When I looked up, there stood a guy with an irresistible smile, his hand unmistakably extended in my direction. Only in my dreams had anyone so attractive ever asked me to dance. I was awestruck and pretty much speechless, but words came easily for him as we glided across the floor. He said his name was Eric, and after a few dances he asked if I wanted to go with him to the refreshment table. By then I wanted to go with him *wherever* he was going!

As we danced the evening away, I felt like Cinderella who had found her Prince Charming. Eric was smart, athletic, gentle, innocent, and funny. He told me he loved sports, and he also played the guitar and sang in a band with some friends. Before we parted, he memorized my phone number and promised to call me.

After I got home, I sat on the end of Janell's bed and raved to her about my magical evening. When I got around to telling her Prince Charming's name, I was surprised to learn that she already knew him. She agreed that he was indeed one of the coolest guys in the school, but she wondered if I realized that he was only a sophomore.

What? Was that even possible? He seemed so much more mature, both physically and mentally, than the other guys I had dated who were my own age and even older. She had to be mistaken.

But the next day when Eric called, he confirmed what Janell had told me. He was indeed a sophomore and was two years younger than I was. He couldn't even drive at night yet! Logically, a romantic relationship should have been out of the question, but like many young lovers, I was not about to let logic overrule my passion.

Later, Eric and I talked at length about the difference in our ages, and he assured me it didn't bother him at all. For myself, I was happy to go against the social norm if it meant being with him. Another girl in our school had already been dating a younger guy for several months, and they seemed to be handling everything just fine. I was absolutely thrilled to be joining ranks with her.

The more time I spent with Eric, the more enchanted I became. The entire world seemed to be drawn to him. Adults, children, peers, the elderly—everyone adored him. His charming nature exceeded my wildest dreams and easily won the favor of my parents, my sisters, and even my brother. When Eric asked me to go steady, I was ecstatic.

Though we were together often, it was never enough for me. I loved it when he waited outside my classroom door and walked me to my next class. Sometimes we had lunch together, but he often went home or ate with his friends. He practiced with his band several evenings during the week and he usually had football practice right after school. Though I'd never had any interest in football before, I was suddenly going to every game. I went to his band performances whenever I could even though I didn't get much time alone with him. Watching him from the sidelines was better than being anywhere else without him.

Eric rode his motorcycle to my house on Saturday afternoons. The minute my little sisters heard the roar of his bike coming down the lane, they would race outside, grab his hands, and jubilantly lead him into the house to find me. He willingly joined in any task we might be doing, playfully teasing my mom and engaging my little sisters. He always jumped in to help me wash dishes or hang wet laundry on the clothesline in the backyard. I was totally living my dream, and I could not have been happier . . . except for the nagging fear that Eric might discover I wasn't as wonderful as he thought.

Even though he appeared to be as smitten as I was, my fearful thoughts wouldn't leave me alone to enjoy our relationship. I desperately wanted to be the perfect girlfriend for him—cute enough, skinny enough, smart enough, talented enough, clever enough—"enough" of everything to keep him and this incredible feeling in my life forever. Would I really be able to avoid losing him to some cuter, skinnier girl?

After going steady for a few months, Eric and I began talking about marriage. We knew the conversation was premature, but waiting several years to marry my dream boy didn't seem like a sacrifice. The only thing that mattered was the promise of his love. He wasn't a member of my church yet, but he liked going to activities with me. He said he wanted to join our church as soon as he turned eighteen and no longer needed his parents' consent. We talked about serving missions at the same time before getting married in the temple. We even chose names for our future children. Nothing made me happier than discussing long-term plans with Eric.

At the end of our dates Eric and I usually engaged in some passionate kissing, but if the lights were still on in the kitchen, he liked to go in and chat with my mom. She often worked on a wedding cake at night since she had recently added professional cake decorating to her long list of talents. Mother was always delighted to see Eric. They would laugh and joke with each other as we snacked on the slivers of cake she had trimmed from her latest masterpiece. I was in heaven as I watched him becoming part of my world. No previous boyfriend had so totally won the approval of my family.

But after Eric and I shared our final goodnight kiss and the sound of his motorcycle faded in the distance, my blissful state quickly changed to despair as my thoughts turned to the cake I had just eaten. What had I been thinking? Why was I so weak? How could I have allowed myself to eat that stuff when I was supposed to be getting skinny so Eric would never stop loving me? My daily weigh-ins had begun to reflect my lack of willpower, and I was terrified that Eric might reject me.

Night after night Mother listened to me wail about my weight. Finally one night, after a particularly dramatic expression of my remorse, she responded in exasperation, "Well, if you feel that bad about it, go stick your finger down your throat and get rid of it!" That grabbed my attention. I'd never heard of such a thing.

She explained that when something she had eaten made her feel sick, she drank some warm water and made herself throw up. She said it always made her feel better. Wow! Deliberately making myself vomit sounded totally gross, but when I thought about it, it didn't seem nearly as bad as the possibility of losing Eric. I decided to give it a try.

Stimulating my gag response was surprisingly easy. The cake hadn't had time to sour in my stomach, so the experience wasn't as unpleasant as I had expected. It was a great relief to know that this time I wouldn't gain any extra weight even though I had just eaten way too much cake.

Suddenly, the solution to my problem appeared to be simple and painless. Ingenious, really! If I couldn't make myself stay on my diet, I now had a way to avoid the consequences of my overeating!

Unbeknownst to me, this would be a defining moment in my life. Like the first drink or the first cigarette that leads someone down an unexpected path of addiction, I naively crossed a line and was immediately hooked. This single choice would have a profound impact on my life for many years to come. My emotional vulnerability, my youth, my past experiences, my perfectionistic yearning for control, all combined in a perfect storm to create a seven-year prison sentence. After that first fateful night, it quickly became impossible for me to break free.

Even though my mother introduced me to intentional purging, she is certainly not to blame for the path I chose. Bulimia was not a commonly known problem at that point. I was miserable, and she did her best to help me feel better. The path I unwittingly chose eventually proved to be one of my greatest teachers in life. It taught me many lessons about fear and love, about human needs, about God, and about perfectionism. It gave me more compassion and understanding than I could ever have gained from reading a whole library of books, or from simply observing the pain of others. My journey has convinced me that God intends for *all* our life experiences to work together for our good.

A few nights after that first experience, when I had once again eaten way too much cake, I found it even easier to make myself throw up. After a few subsequent nights of emptying my stomach, my mother knocked on the bathroom door and warned me that I shouldn't make up-chucking a regular practice. It was an awkward moment, but I knew she was right. I'd already begun to feel guilty for wasting so much food.

Despite her warning and my increasing guilt, I continued to find myself thinking I absolutely had to throw up "just this one last time." After dinner each night, I would spread my books out and do my homework on the kitchen table. When everyone else was in bed, I'd slip into the bathroom and throw up as quietly as possible. It was tricky because I wanted to avoid another confrontation with my mother, but if I waited too long, the vomit was foul and would burn my throat. Unpleasant as it was, I always felt compelled to go on. My vision of the perfect body was at stake.

Without a clue of where this secretive path might lead, I rejoiced wildly in the freedom and hope it brought me. I was free from the fear of gaining weight, and I was confident that Eric's love would increase as I became skinnier and more attractive. I ignored the troubling feeling that I really wasn't free at all as I once again embarked on the shadowy path of telling one lie to cover another.

As the pounds melted away, compliments flowed to me from every direction. My stomach became perfectly flat, my thighs no longer rubbed together, and my body fit into much smaller clothing. My improved appearance became the topic of conversation with everyone who knew me, and the praise was wonderfully intoxicating.

To my surprise, Eric was totally unimpressed. He said he was okay with my new look, but he actually preferred the old me. Really, how could that be? I was certain he would have changed his mind if I had kept gaining weight, and I felt grateful I'd found a temporary way to halt the consequences of eating all that cake at night. Surely I would soon be strong enough to gain control since I was loved by the most awesome boy in the school.

But my willpower did not increase. In fact, it seemed to become weaker and weaker, and a recurring cycle quickly developed. My firm resolves to never throw up again were followed by brief periods of hope and strict dieting. However, within a short time—usually just a couple of days—I would find myself eating more than I had planned, and my fear of being fat and rejected would take over. Though my intention was to be strong and exercise magnificent willpower in the face of temptation, after having eaten too much, I always concluded that the only option *at that point* was to throw up "one last time."

Each time I embraced this lie, my mind would become numb and I would eat with unrestrained abandon. It no longer mattered how much I ate, because I didn't have to live with the consequences. I felt like I'd somehow stepped out of my body and someone else had taken over, like I was driving a crazy runaway vehicle, deliberately pushing on the gas pedal when I knew I should be stomping on the brake.

As soon as my stomach was uncomfortably engorged, the reality of making myself throw up had to be faced. Angry, condemning self-talk would flood my mind as I struggled to accomplish my disgusting task in complete secrecy. I'd rant on and on about how stupid and weak I was, chiding myself that I would never be good enough for God if I didn't somehow get my act together. After my stomach was empty, however, my mood would change. Sunshine would burst through the darkness for a moment and I would feel relieved, contrite, and hopeful. In that state of mind, it seemed totally reasonable to promise God I would never ever let this happen again.

And thus, the cycle continued.

# 6

# RAIN, RAIN, GO AWAY!

*Breaking up is hard to do*

Although I loved having a skinnier body, I hated living a life of deception. I did my best to skirt probing questions about how I'd lost all the weight, but sometimes there was no alternative to out-and-out lying since disclosing the truth was not an option. I rationalized that the lies didn't really matter in this case because I planned to quit throwing up immediately.

My self-worth depended almost completely on Eric, but also on my academic success. Ignoring my body's plea for more sleep, I pressed forward, obsessing over my relationship, my homework, and my eating disorder. It wasn't easy to juggle all the demands, but I had a skinny body, an awesome boyfriend, and a perfect GPA—everything I thought I really wanted.

Then tragedy struck. Eric's parents decided we were too involved, and they said if he didn't break up with me they wouldn't allow him to ride his motorcycle or play in his band. When Eric told me, I panicked, but he quickly assured me of his enduring love and his commitment to our future. He promised he'd secretly visit me as often as he could, and said he'd get his own place as soon as he turned eighteen so we could be openly together again. Of course, I rejoiced at his words because our relationship meant everything to me, but I was now saddled with another secret to guard.

Eric kept his promise. He found many opportunities to come by after his evening activities. To make our secret meetings less obvious, he started dating a girl who lived up the valley from me. That way he could stop by my house on his way home without raising suspicion. During these stolen moments, he showered me with the attention I craved, always apologizing for his absence in my life. My parents didn't say much, but I knew they were concerned.

Eric stopped by particularly late one night. Everyone else in the house was asleep, but he had told me he was planning to come, so I anxiously waited. When he finally arrived, I happily sank into the tenderness of his embrace. Drenched in the intoxication of our closeness, my carefully defined boundaries became a little fuzzy. We allowed ourselves to be more passionate than we had ever been before, but fortunately, he didn't stay long enough to really test my boundaries.

The next time I saw Eric, he fumbled for words as he attempted to apologize for his inappropriate behavior. I could tell he was uncomfortable, and I wanted to make things easier for him. Rather than accepting his apology and acknowledging my own responsibility, I foolishly pretended that I didn't know what he was talking about. Perfectionists hate to be wrong, and I mistakenly thought I could somehow protect both of us from feeling wrong if I simply denied the truth.

My game playing didn't help at all. In fact, it increased the awkwardness. It complicated his apology and kept the focus on his offense rather than letting it go so we could move on. It's the only time I remember Eric getting upset with me. As soon as I realized he was agitated, I hastily backtracked, accepted his apology, and humbly offered my own. Once again, he expressed his undying love for me and pledged his commitment to our relationship.

However, a secret life always takes its toll. Soon I began to feel a sense of restlessness in Eric's visits. I couldn't imagine life without him, and I desperately tried to believe the excuses he gave for dropping by less frequently. But the writing was on the wall. The tide had turned, and for him, the thrill of our relationship was over.

One cold Monday morning, I opened my school locker and an avalanche of envelopes and boxes spilled onto my feet. In a split second, I realized I was staring at every card, every picture, every gift I had ever given Eric. Overwhelming pain slammed my chest as I surveyed the mound that represented his undeniable rejection. Trapped in slow motion, I dropped to the floor and gathered the evidence of the reality I had refused to accept.

Struggling to conceal my grief, I stuffed everything back into my locker and ran down the hall to the bathroom. My perfect dream was shattered. My life had lost its purpose. It was impossible for me to contain my tears.

When the bell rang for first period, I stayed in the bathroom, too buried in grief to go to class. When the bell rang again an hour later, I still hadn't managed to pull myself together. I hid in a stall until the tardy bell for the next class cleared the students from the bathroom and hallways.

I knew I wouldn't be able to hide in the bathroom all day, so I calmed myself the best I could, splashed cold water on my face, and hurried to the office to call my mom. When she heard the pain in my voice, she came to get me without asking any questions. I sobbed all the way home, unable to compose an intelligible explanation, and I spent the next five days in bed crying my heart out.

My mother and younger sisters mourned right along with me, although not as dramatically as I did. I felt I had failed each of them as well as myself. We would miss so many things about Eric. No longer would there be a reason to listen for the roar of a motorcycle coming down the lane, or to anticipate his mischievous eyes and charming half-grin at our front door. The only positive thing I could see from our break-up was that I hardly ate anything that whole week, and even though I didn't throw up once, I still lost five pounds.

Since our high school was small, there was no way to avoid seeing Eric when I went back to school the next week. For the first few days, I went out of my way to run into him hoping it had again been his parents' idea rather than his own. But his desire to completely disconnect was reaffirmed when I repeatedly saw him holding hands with a cute little skinny blonde girl. The thought of them being together tormented me, and seeing them in the hallway sent me running to the bathroom in tears time after time.

I didn't know how to let go of my attachment to Eric even if I had wanted to. Catching a glimpse of him without his new girlfriend sent me hopefully fantasizing about us getting back together. But then I'd see them together with his arm wrapped affectionately around her and the torture would start all over again.

My life felt like such a nightmare that I finally arranged to spend the summer in Utah with my grandmother. As soon as school got out, I would go to Salt Lake City, find a job, and work until I had to leave for college. That way I would avoid any possibility of bumping into Eric and his girlfriend.

Since I could no longer rely on Eric's affection for my self-worth, my drive for academic success increased. I was named valedictorian of our graduating class and was awarded several small scholarships. Though I loved the recognition and praise, in my heart I felt undeserving. I knew some of my classmates were smarter than I was. A couple of teachers even made pointed comments about how those students would have been in my place if they had only applied themselves a little.

My English teacher, who had been hired that year to infuse the school with fresh ideas and innovative thinking, validated my sense of worthlessness after reviewing my valedictory speech. He said it was a good Sunday sermon, but was far beneath the commanding address I should be delivering as valedictorian. I was embarrassed and humiliated, but I had no vision for improving it. Besides, I didn't have the energy to rewrite my speech even if I had known what to say.

Just keeping my eating disorder a secret was becoming more and more exhausting. Though I desperately wanted to live up to all the expectations, I saw myself failing on every side—failing God, failing myself, failing the entire world. I felt completely powerless to straighten things out and make them right. The only thing that got me through those last few weeks was the knowledge that it would all be over soon.

A few hours after delivering my unimpressive valedictory speech, I was on a train racing through the night toward my grandmother's house in Salt Lake City. While my classmates were celebrating at an all-night graduation party, I was doing my best to escape my broken heart and my broken past. I tried to put all the pain behind and visualize the new, exciting life awaiting me. Maybe I would meet someone who would make me forget all about Eric.

During the train ride I also earnestly prayed, promising God I would never throw up again. I thought this change of scene would be all I needed to leave my problems behind. In my new environment, I would surely become the beautiful, desirable, skinny, in-control person I dreamed of being. This new beginning would allow me to forsake all my secrets, my pain, and my failure.

I settled into the extra bedroom of my grandmother's house feeling nervous and excited. Since I had always thought it would be cool to live in the city, I was eager to explore my new surroundings. My uncle, who lived within a few miles of my grandmother, came to my aid. He taught me how to use the city bus system, helped me search the newspaper for job possibilities, and took me to my interview at a local hospital where I was immediately hired as secretary on the pediatrics floor.

The next day I caught the bus just a few blocks from my grandmother's house and was at work in twenty minutes. The girl in charge was pleasant and encouraging as she showed me around and explained my responsibilities. The job felt intimidating, but the staff generously complimented my work from the moment I started. The praise was exhilarating, and I managed to make it through the first week without throwing up at all. I felt strong and hopeful!

But no matter how far you run, you can't run away from yourself. I desperately missed having a social life to distract me from my insecurities. My grandmother's ward was made up entirely of widows and older couples, so it provided no opportunity to meet young people. The women I worked with at the hospital were kind, but they were all older and didn't invite me into their well-established circles. Even though I had promised myself and God I would never throw up again, when my insecurity about my work combined with my loneliness, fear, and perfectionism, food again became the answer to my pain.

Though it had been less than six months since that fateful night when I first chose to throw up, I now felt totally powerless to resist the spell. Once again I found myself locking the bathroom door behind me and doing everything I could to disguise the sounds of my vomiting. I was beyond disgusted with myself. Why was I sabotaging this perfect opportunity to fix my life? It made no sense at all.

Eventually I gave up on solving my problem that summer and convinced myself I would be able to muster greater willpower once I got to college. For the time being, I decided I should focus my attention on my relationship with my grandmother since I didn't know her very well. I admired the special bond between her and my dad, and I wanted her to think he had raised the perfect daughter.

My grandmother and I did indeed share some lovely hours reading, singing, and playing the piano together, but deception always exacts a price. The guilt and shame I felt for trying to impress her, while at the same time secretly throwing up the food she so kindly prepared for me, created a barrier between us that I simply could not overcome.

Near the end of the summer, my family came to pick me up, and we all rode the train to California to visit my mother's sister and her family. It was an awesome trip. My aunt fed us waffles topped with ice cream and cherry pie filling. We piled in the back of my uncle's pickup, and he took us to the beach. Another day we went to Disneyland. That week was a wonderful distraction from all the stress in my life.

After our vacation, it was time to pack my bags, head to the University of Idaho, and put the past behind me. Convinced that everything would be different, I was excited to jump into this new chapter of my life. At the university I would be surrounded by people my own age, there would be lots of guys to date, and I would be so busy with school and social activities that I would never look back. Surely the clouds that had followed me to Salt Lake City would be left far behind.

# 7

# PERSISTENT STORMS

*Confessions alone can't cure an eating disorder*

When I checked in at the dorm, a girl with long, honey-colored hair hurried toward me. She flashed a disarming smile and introduced herself as Julie Vincent. She said I was her roommate, and she'd been anxiously watching for me. She grabbed my heaviest suitcase and led me down the main floor hallway to our room, pointing out the bathroom and showers we would be sharing with twenty other girls.

Julie had a bubbly personality and we chatted comfortably as she helped me unpack. She had grown up in the western part of the state and her high school was about the same size as mine. I was surprised when she told me she'd been on the drill team because even though she was cute, she definitely wasn't skinny. Her boyfriend had been their school's star basketball player and would be playing basketball on the university team.

Before arriving at the university, I had been encouraged to make the LDS Institute of Religion the center of my social life. As soon as I learned Julie was a member of my church, we quickly finished unpacking my things and set out on our first adventure to the Institute. Unfortunately, when we got there we found it quite deserted. Even though we poked around a little, we couldn't find a list of upcoming activities. All we came up with was a schedule of classes. Of course I planned to attend at least one religion class each semester, but I was much more interested in the schedule of social activities. My roommate already had her impressive man, and I was anxious to find an awesome guy I could claim as my own.

Because my funds were limited, I had signed up to live in a cooperative dorm. That meant I got a discount on my room and board in exchange for weekly kitchen and cleaning duties. During our dorm orientation, I discovered it also meant I had access to a huge refrigerator where the leftovers were made available to everyone. I immediately realized this arrangement could be a big problem for me, so I vowed I would never set foot in that kitchen except to fulfill my assigned tasks.

Unfortunately, my willpower was no match for the constant beckoning of that refrigerator. I had practiced my stress response so well that when college life proved to be stressful from the very first day of class, I knew right where to go. Of course, I now realize that fridge or no fridge, I would have been driven to find food somewhere. It just wouldn't have been as convenient.

The dining hall, which doubled as our study hall, was in the basement right next to the kitchen. A door off to the right opened into a short hallway with two sleeping rooms and another bathroom. When I went downstairs to study at night, I would promise myself I absolutely wasn't going to step even a toe into that kitchen, but my mind was already riveted on those leftovers. Rarely was I able to resist.

I tried to eat as inconspicuously as possible, but occasionally someone would say something like, "Wow, you actually eat a *lot* for someone who's so skinny!" Or they would ask, "How can you eat so much and not gain weight?" Hoping to avoid telling an out and out lie, I would make some vague comment about a high metabolism and then quickly change the subject.

When I was sick of trying to study, or sick of myself for stuffing my face again, I would slip into the basement bathroom and empty my stomach as discreetly as I could. I was always on the alert for footsteps, but since that bathroom only serviced two dorm rooms, my retching was most often uninterrupted.

When Julie later broke up with her boyfriend, my life became even more complicated. With extra time on her hands, Julie often asked me to do something with her, but many times I had already committed myself to a date with the toilet bowl. I wanted to go with her, but instead I struggled to invent acceptable excuses so she would leave me to indulge in the thing I hated most about myself.

My life was again an endless cycle of fervent promises, followed by periods of near-starvation—which I interpreted as progress—followed by frenzied bingeing and purging. I always told myself I was going to start eating normally, but by that time, I no longer knew what "normal" really was. Any amount of food seemed like too much.

Though my binge and purge cycle continued to plague me, there were positive aspects of college life. The part I liked best was the social life. Indeed, it exceeded my expectations. I frequently had more invitations to go out with guys than I could fit into my weekend. Whenever I had to turn someone down, I expressed sincere regret and encouraged him to call again.

I did my best to hone my dating skills according to the charm books that my dorm mates passed around, but my efforts were mostly designed to keep the guys interested in me rather than learning how to show genuine interest in them. Lost in myself, I had few relationships that endured beyond a couple of weeks, but having a lot of dates gave me a reprieve from the stress of schoolwork, the endless self-loathing, and the feeling of worthlessness.

I longed, I yearned, I ached to be free of the monster that held my life hostage, but I had no idea how to break the bonds by myself, and I couldn't imagine asking anyone for help. I was certain everyone would withdraw from me in disgust if they knew. And I didn't blame them. I truly wished I could withdraw from myself!

Thoughts that I was failing my church constantly beset me. How could I claim to be a follower of Christ when my life felt like one big, ugly lie? I began to wonder how I might end my life so that I could be free of the tangled web I had created. It had been so easy to get into this mess, but now there seemed to be no way out.

At the end of my first semester, I was studying for my final psychology exam when I felt a slight pain in my abdomen. At first, I thought it was just a stomach ache from the pizza I had eaten earlier, but the pain became so severe my roommate insisted we go to the emergency room. I wondered if I might be lucky enough to die that night, but the next morning found me waking up from an appendectomy rather than in a mortuary or taking my psychology exam.

Around noon they transferred me to the student infirmary. When I arrived, I weighed myself on the scale in the hallway and was excited to discover I had lost three pounds. My stomach seemed particularly flat even with the bandage covering the incision. Maybe I was finally going to be skinny enough to be happy!

When the nurse brought in my lunch tray, my excitement suddenly turned to distress. I was famished, but I didn't want to eat anything. What if I regained that wonderful weight loss? The doctor had told me to limit my activity for a few weeks and I feared I wouldn't be able to maintain this lower weight if I ate a normal meal.

After deliberating for a while, I decided my body probably needed nourishment since it had just been through a surgery. However, a few bites later, I began to worry that I had already eaten too much. Though I suspected that throwing up could rupture my incision, that risk felt much less distressing than the risk of regaining three pounds of ugly fat. Consequently, I finished everything on my tray, drank some warm water, shut myself in the bathroom, and quickly emptied my stomach.

Since the purging didn't seem to hurt anything, I decided to try a few sit-ups. When I found they caused no pain, I did a few more later that day and continued to increase the number throughout my recovery. My stomach became amazingly flat. I had never been so skinny and I was elated. Fortunately I experienced no adverse consequences from that foolishness.

Back in the dorms I skipped meals and avoided the refrigerator. Physically I felt weak and hungry, but emotionally I felt successful and powerful. That feeling lasted only until I realized I was now facing the rigorous workload of a new semester on top of my finals from the previous semester. Suddenly I was again bowing to the porcelain bowl.

Suicidal thoughts filled my head, but I didn't actively pursue them. First of all, I was terrified of dying, and second, I couldn't think of anything I might be strong enough to follow through with. Perhaps the most deterring factor, though, was the heartbreak I knew it would cause my dad. It undoubtedly would have devastated my whole family, but my father was so sensitive that I feared the choice to take my own life might break his heart and literally cause him to die.

I spent a lot of time lost in the "if only" mindset. "If only I had never started throwing up. If only I had someone to talk to. If only I had never been born! Then I wouldn't be in this pain, and I wouldn't be able to hurt anybody else either." Over and over I wished I could just evaporate into thin air, leaving no trace and no pain behind.

Somewhere along the way, I picked up the belief that if I could only make myself humble enough, God would forgive me and fix me. Consequently, I made a desperate attempt to demonstrate complete humility when I prayed. To me, that meant convincing God that I recognized how evil my sins truly were, and I understood and accepted my total worthlessness. Since my problem persisted, I assumed I needed to be even more humble to merit God's help, but I couldn't figure out what more to say or how to feel more contrite.

My prayers were as honest and sincere as I knew how to make them. "Heavenly Father, please help me," I'd beg. "I can't stop this insane deception without some help. I know you hate me because I am so pathetic and weak. I know I am repulsive and worthless to you. I keep asking you to forgive me for being so wicked, and I keep promising you that I will change, but I never do. So, of course, you know that I am just a big liar, and I really can't blame you for not wanting to help me."

Though I didn't realize it at the time, the words of my prayers were actually closing my heart to God's healing power. I wouldn't allow myself to believe that He could love me or that He would want to help me in my messy, broken state. After all, I reasoned, God is pure, and no unclean thing can enter His presence, so why would He care about me in my hideous state of filthiness?

I now understand how distorted and ineffective this kind of self-punishment is, whether offered as a prayer or simply repeated in negative self-talk. I love sharing God's message of unfailing love for each of His children, and His eternal desire to rescue us from our pain, whether self-inflicted or otherwise. At that time, however, my despair and self-loathing continued to mount until I felt like I was losing my mind. I finally decided I had to either die or get help. Since suicide was out of the question and acute appendicitis hadn't killed me, I searched my mind for someone I could divulge my repulsive secret to.

As a teen, I had been taught that we should confess serious offenses to the bishop, but I couldn't even imagine revealing my messy problem to Bishop Jensen. His meticulous appearance and efficient manner oozed of self-discipline. But I was desperate and I couldn't come up with a better option, so I finally contacted his secretary and made an appointment.

In the days before my appointment, I spent many hours writing and rewriting a letter. Since I knew I'd have a hard time expressing my thoughts once we were face to face in his office, I poured my heart onto the paper, detailing at length the hopelessness of my situation. I told him I understood my total lack of worthiness, calling myself a worthless thief, and a wickedly deceitful person. I even suggested he should remove my name from the church membership records.

Getting to that appointment seriously tested my resolve, but I forced myself to go because I was so desperate for the pain and the craziness to end. I barely breathed as Bishop Jensen began reading the nine hand-written pages I had carefully composed. As the agonizing minutes ticked away, I waited for his expressionless face to take on a look of horror or disgust.

My hands ached to snatch the letter back from him. My mind wanted me to scream, "Never mind! Just never mind!" My feet wanted to run from his office, to run from all the fear and frustration and pain, to run from my whole miserable existence. But I knew there was nowhere to run. I was in his office because I had already tried running, and nothing had changed.

I have no idea what went through my bishop's mind, but when he spoke, his words were gentle and kind. He clearly desired to help me, and he assured me of God's love regardless of the things I had done. He counseled me to turn to Christ for help and encouraged me to fill my life with good things so I wouldn't have time to indulge in food. Unlike bishops today, he wasn't equipped with contact information for addiction recovery programs, support groups, and counseling. Still, my appointment with him gave me hope. I had thought I would die of embarrassment, but instead, my burden felt light, and I went home feeling wonderfully relieved, having confessed all. I was sure I was at last on the road to freedom.

For the next several days, I followed my bishop's advice and stuffed my schedule instead of my face. I hardly ate anything and I reveled in the sense of power it gave me to deny my hunger pains. But that delicious feeling of control lasted less than a week. Though I obediently buried myself in schoolwork, music, my social life, and a sewing project, I simply couldn't stay busy enough to forget about food.

My anxiety increased because now I found myself avoiding my bishop. Whenever he caught me unaware and asked that trite old question, "How are you doing?" I was sure what he really meant was, "Have you been throwing up again?" I couldn't admit to him that I was still hopelessly stuck. His previous compassion would surely turn to disgust if he learned I had done nothing but waste his time. I didn't want him to think his kindness hadn't been enough. I knew he wasn't the problem. It was all about me being so pathetic and worthless.

As the tedious days of school, and the long, anxious nights of eating and throwing up wore on into my second year of college, the scales began telling a different story. My body was adjusting to the abuse, and the numbers began to creep upward despite my diligent purging. My constant disgust and self-hatred rekindled thoughts of suicide, and once again I tried to think of someone to help me, but who could I possibly turn to now?

Eventually, I decided to call my religion teacher. He was light-hearted in class sometimes and I had always felt more comfortable talking to him than my bishop. I desperately hoped exposing my ugly secret for a second time would prove to God I was finally humble enough that he could now intervene and fix my life. Again I entered the interview with great fear and trembling. Although I didn't write a letter this time, my profuse tears and my expressions of self-hatred clearly communicated my remorse and my sense of worthlessness.

After listening to my story, my teacher reminded me of God's love for all of His children. He even mocked me a little for being worried about what everyone would think if they knew. He said I was being egotistical to think people were constantly thinking about me. Then he told me I wasn't really as bad as

I imagined, and he reminded me that everyone was struggling with something. To illustrate his point, he confessed to me a serious sin that he was currently trying to overcome. I had no idea how to respond, so I just sat there in shock.

When I left his office, I felt relieved for having confessed my secret, but as I continued to reflect on our conversation, I felt more and more embarrassed that he thought I was egotistical. And I also felt deeply troubled by *his* confession. He had been my guiding light, and even though I didn't want to be judgmental, his secret kept bothering me.

My confession obviously didn't do what I had hoped, because in a few days, I fell back into my familiar cycle of eating and throwing up, once again engulfed in despair and self-loathing. Though I still craved the association of other students at the Institute, I began to carefully avoid my teacher, not only because he knew my dark secrets, but because I felt awkward knowing one of his.

My last confession at the university was definitely the most extreme. This confession wasn't exactly voluntary, and it certainly wasn't private like the other two had been. It was initiated by a note I found taped to the door of the downstairs bathroom stall where I most often went to throw up. The note simply stated, "Whoever is using our bathroom as a garbage can for your stomach, stop it!"

I was horrified! Though the note didn't specify my name, my secret was obviously out. Fear and guilt overwhelmed me as I considered what it meant. I had always been so careful to enter the bathroom when no one was around, to be as silent as humanly possible, to stop throwing up if I heard footsteps in the hallway, and to carefully wipe down everything so as to leave no trace. I had chosen to believe that no one suspected, but now the undeniable truth stared me in the face. Even with my best efforts, I had failed.

After accepting the fact that my secret was out to some of my housemates, I came to the conclusion that I needed to admit my guilt to all of them. From my distorted way of thinking, I reasoned that since I had been stealing leftovers from everyone, I should apologize to everyone. Complete humiliation before my whole dorm seemed the appropriate punishment to fit the crime, and I thought it would surely be painful enough to make me quit overeating and throwing up.

At the end of the next dorm meeting, I stood and announced that I had something I needed to say to everyone. That I didn't die of fright right there on the spot is no small miracle. My knees barely supported me and my head seemed lost in another world. My face and ears burned as I stammered out something about how hopeless I was and repeatedly apologized for abusing bathrooms, stealing food, and in general, for being a worthless and disgusting person. When I finally quit rambling, an awkward silence followed, and then gradually gave way to muffled whispers.

A few girls approached me and said they accepted my apology, admired my courage, and wished me success. Others weren't so kind. I tried not to care about the disparaging glances and the uncensored comments that reached my ears. The only thing that mattered was my secret was out, and I was finally free—or so I thought.

A few days later I began making stealthy visits to the basement bathroom of the dorm next door. That bathroom seemed to be occupied way more often than the one in my dorm, so many nights I was forced to brave the darkness and walk up the hill to the next closest bathroom. It happened to be in a practice hall for music majors, so my miserable retching was often accompanied by a moaning cello or a mournful French horn. Their sorrowful tones were a perfect match for the anguish and despair I felt over my hopeless situation.

Earlier that year, a prominent church leader had come to visit the LDS Institute at the university. He'd given a talk about the power of our desires and said if we truly wanted something, we would do whatever it took to make it happen. I felt like I truly wanted to stop all the bingeing, purging, and lying. I sincerely wanted my life to be different, and I had done everything I could think of to make a fresh start. Why did I continue to fail? What was I missing? How could I make this raging storm pass?

# 8

# MORE DISTURBANCES ON THE RADAR

*Missionary service and doctors' visits
don't cure eating disorders*

When the semester ended, I moved in with a family who offered to trade my summer room and board for house cleaning and ironing. The wife was an exceptional cook who placed tantalizing meals before us every evening. She and her husband welcomed me warmly into their home, asking about the details of my childhood, and sharing stories of their exciting adventures in faraway countries.

The family was so gracious that I desperately wanted to reciprocate, but my life was too out of control. Each night I would sneak into the kitchen and forage for leftovers, hoping that the wife would assume her son or her husband was consuming the missing food. The guilt was formidable, but the urge was irresistible. Every day was laden with stress over it, and I breathed a huge sigh of relief when I left their home at the end of the summer without having been caught or confronted.

That fall I roomed with two girls I had met at church. Our apartment was a couple of miles from the university, and I hoped that walking would help me lose the weight I had started to regain. I got a part-time job on campus and spent my free hours studying in the library so I wouldn't be around food. I tried to avoid buying anything that invited me to binge, but all my efforts had little effect. In the evening I always found something to stuff into my mouth.

Since I found no pleasure in the taste of the food, it didn't really matter what I ate. Sometimes I'd whip up an inexpensive cake mix or a batch of pancakes. Sometimes I ate my roommates' food, all the while rationalizing that I would replace it the next day so it wasn't really stealing. Of course, I would randomly rearrange everything in the fridge or the cupboard hoping to make it less obvious that I had "borrowed" something without permission.

Praise for my academic excellence ended after my second semester because my grades slipped to include a couple of B's. Since dating was pretty much my only source of relief from my pain, I desperately sought male companionship wherever I could find it. And it wasn't usually hard to find.

Most of the majors offered at the University of Idaho were of much greater interest to men than to women, so there was no shortage of men. I preferred to date guys who went to the Institute, but if someone else asked me out I most often accepted. And I wasn't particularly careful about the reputation of those I went out with, or the places I allowed them to take me. More than once I found myself in a situation that could have easily turned into a disaster.

When I look back, I am overwhelmed with gratitude that I didn't end up an abandoned, unwed mother. It could have happened so easily. The drive to ease the pain of perfectionism through physical affection is compelling. We happily accept the counterfeit love we are offered, ignoring the risk of being stranded in an immensely life-altering situation.

By the time I started my junior year, my body had completely adapted to its state of starvation. Though my daily purging continued, losing even a fraction of a pound became nearly impossible. In fact, over the course of that year, I gained about thirty pounds, stabilizing a few pounds over my original high school weight. No matter how diligently I purged, my ability to control the scale was gone.

Interestingly enough, I had two of my most enduring relationships during that time. The first was with Jeff, a tall, dark, jaw-droppingly handsome young man who was an excellent student and a celebrated college athlete. He had recently been disowned by his family because he had joined the Church, and I loved talking with him about the doctrines, practices, and policies that were new to him.

My lingering feelings for Eric faded as my affection for Jeff grew, and before long we were talking about marriage. I blissfully envisioned myself as the perfect wife for him, and fervently promised to rid my life of my secret eating disorder. When nothing changed, I agonized over what I should do. I felt I either had to break the cycle or find the courage to tell Jeff about it so he wouldn't be shocked by it after we married. However, my concern became a moot point a few months later when Jeff apologetically told me he was being unfair to me because he was still in love with his former girlfriend, Nancy.

I was crushed, and for a while, I continued to hope that Jeff would change his mind. Of course, when he showed me a picture of Nancy, I understood perfectly. Nancy was wonderfully skinny and petite. Just a year earlier I had been at least as skinny as she was, but now I wallowed in extra pounds and extra misery, convincing myself that Jeff would have given me his heart if I hadn't regained those thirty pounds of ugliness.

The second relationship was with a guy who made such a fuss over me that I truly felt treasured by him. He didn't seem to care about my weight at all. He was thoughtful, funny, and generous, though not breathtakingly handsome like Jeff had been. After several months of steady dating, he asked me to marry him. I was totally flattered but I knew I wasn't in love with him. I wondered if I might eventually fall in love if we continued to date, but even so, there was no way I could tell him about my eating disorder when he thought I was such a perfect catch. I was sure if I told him he would reject me, so I chose to reject him.

Besides, I wasn't sure I wanted to get married yet. Even though my life was a disaster, in the back of my mind I still entertained the possibility of going on a mission. I was definitely ready for a break from school, and I knew my parents would be pleased if I went. I also had great hopes that serving a mission would prove to God I was worthy to have Him fix my messed-up life.

A few months before the semester ended, I met with Bishop Jensen to talk about the possibility of going on a mission. He heartily praised my desire to serve and enthusiastically related some of his own mission experiences. I hoped he wouldn't bring up my eating disorder, but as the interview was drawing to a close he looked me straight in the eye and asked if I had been able to conquer it.

Deeply embarrassed, I admitted I hadn't really made any progress. He told me I needed to work harder to get it under control and sternly warned me not to marry until I had mastered it because it would "lead to marital problems and to taking food out of [my] children's mouths." The fire of shame burned bright red on my face and I feared he would say I shouldn't go on a mission, but he handed me the necessary application and medical forms and told me to get them back to him as soon as possible.

Even though my boyfriend really wanted me to stay home and marry him, he also wanted me to feel his love, so he totally supported my preparations. He drove me to most of my dental and doctor appointments for the required exams and vaccinations, and when he wasn't available to go with me, he had me take his car. He even went with me to return my completed papers to Bishop Jensen. He was clearly there for me, but he had a hard time sharing in my excitement because he saw his hopes and dreams fading away.

When the semester ended a few weeks later, I packed up my room and made the long drive home. The letter telling me where I would be sent to serve my mission arrived a few days after I did. I remember standing in the kitchen with my family when I eagerly opened it. It said I would be serving in the Central American Mission, which was headquartered in Costa Rica. Though I wasn't sure where that even was, I had set my feet on the path and I wasn't turning back.

We barely had time to gather everything on the mission list, sew a few dresses, and make a quick trip to the Idaho Falls temple before my entry date. By the middle of June, I was attending the Language Training Center in Provo, Utah, located on the Brigham Young University campus. I spent my days attempting to conquer the first couple of missionary discussions in Spanish and cautiously hiding my eating disorder. In spite of my pernicious secret, I treasured my experience there. My companion was wonderfully accepting of everyone and I adored her. She was from Mississippi and her accent played havoc with her Spanish, but her perspective lifted and blessed everyone she interacted with.

Two months later, I found myself in Honduras adjusting to missionary life and haphazardly communicating in Spanish. There was so much to take in, and I fell in love with my new life. The people were friendly, the culture was fascinating, and the church was growing. But once again I was reminded that "wherever you go, there you are."

My hope for a sweeping cure of my eating disorder was quickly dashed. My fears, comparing, and judging continued to trip me up time and time again. Every stressful thought triggered the impulse to eat. The food was a little different from what I was used to, but that didn't stop me from bingeing. The toilets were a little different from what I was used to, but that didn't stop me from purging. Mission rules require companions to stay together day and night, so it was significantly harder to find opportunities to secretly throw up, but the urge was always on the prowl and few days went by without some stolen moment of purging.

I served with ten different companions during my mission. They were all devoted women, and many of them are still cherished friends. Some of them may have suspected my eating disorder, but no one ever confronted me or otherwise mentioned it. I often ached to open up and be honest with them, but I couldn't bring myself to risk the humiliation or the rejection. I muddled through the best I could, never physically alone, but always isolated by my shameful secret.

Despite the complications caused by my eating disorder, I often felt joyful and divinely supported as I served people throughout Central America. It was confusing to feel such intense happiness when my thoughts so often told me my eating disorder made me disgusting and worthless. The roller coaster never stopped, vacillating wildly between glorious feelings of love and joy, and dark feelings of despair and hopelessness.

When people invited us into their homes, they frequently offered us food, even though most of them couldn't really afford to feed us. They considered us impolite if we refused to eat, and they almost always insisted we have seconds. Since I usually couldn't throw up right after these meals, I hopelessly watched as I packed on another fifteen pounds.

Some of the people called me Gordita, a common term of endearment that literally translates to "little fat girl." Since I knew they didn't mean it to be hurtful, I always smiled and acted like it didn't bother me, but in my mind it was one more painful reminder I was gaining weight, and I could do nothing about it.

In the missionary discussions, we taught people our bodies are sacred. We challenged them to live sexually pure lives and to care for their bodies by refraining from unhealthy substances such as tobacco and alcohol. During these lessons I felt like a disgusting hypocrite because I couldn't stop my own compulsive behavior. Whenever anyone was able to make sweeping changes in their lives, I not only felt great admiration, I also felt extremely envious because I had been desperately trying to change my life for years.

Although I planned to return to the University of Idaho in September to finish my degree, just before I came home I learned that Brigham Young University offered an enticing language option. Students with strong language skills could take one upper division Spanish class, pay a fee, and receive credit for all the prerequisite classes. It was a no-brainer! I could get my academic minor out of the way in one fell swoop, and BYU would satisfy my craving for an active social environment until I could return to the University of Idaho. Little did I know how drastically this one decision would change the course of my life.

When I came home from my mission, I felt an even greater urgency to stop the bingeing and purging because I suddenly saw myself standing at the last major crossroad before entering the unbounded "rest of my life." How could I risk taking this nightmare into marriage? I told myself this absolutely had to be the end of my throwing up, and I devised a rigorous schedule that allowed little time for eating, and absolutely no time for purging. Now all I had to do was make myself stick with the schedule.

Full of high hopes and optimistic expectations, I moved into a house that accommodated ten girls. With so many roommates looking over my shoulder, I again thought I would surely be forced to reform. My resolve lasted for about a week, but just as I had experienced over and over throughout the previous six years, my willpower and best intentions were not enough to overcome my obsessive cycle.

Throwing up day after day, night after night left me physically weary and emotionally drained. More than once I woke up on the bathroom floor in the middle of the night having fallen asleep before I could make myself throw up. Because I had convinced myself this was absolutely, positively going to be my big moment of change, my failure was excruciating. I could barely drag myself to class, and wondered how I was going to make it all the way to graduation.

Desperate to get control of my life, I once again gathered my courage and confessed everything to my bishop. He was a wise and tender-hearted man, but he quickly admitted he had no idea how to help me. He recommended that I see a doctor at the student health center, and he even called and made the appointment for me.

Unlike my bishop, Dr. Brinn was abrupt and impersonal. He was impatient with my tears and demanded I get right to the point. A few minutes into my explanation he brusquely interrupted. "This is nothing more than oral masturbation," he stated matter-of-factly. "You're just doing this to relieve stress. When you get married and start having sex, you'll quit."

I was stunned. He may have intended his words to be insightful, but I had felt so much guilt and shame around anything sexual in my life that I could see nothing but oppressive clouds of condemnation. Those five minutes were the beginning and the end of my professional help. I paid my bill in awkward silence, and fled from the building feeling more wicked and hopeless than ever.

# 9

# MOSTLY SUNNY WITH PATCHES OF TURBULENCE

*Finding Mr. Right in the midst of the storm*

My Spanish class consisted almost entirely of returned missionaries who were working toward the extra language credit just as I was. Among them was Monte Shelley, a young man who had served his mission in Argentina. He was fun and flirty, and he always came in and took a seat right next to me.

After a while, I began trying to avoid him because I wanted to connect with some of the other guys in the class, but whenever I started talking to anyone else, he would come over and join in the conversation. It was obvious he was trying to stake a claim, but I was not interested in limiting my options.

A few weeks into the term, Monte invited me to study with him, and I gladly accepted. Even though he wasn't my first choice for a date, he was pleasant to be around, and he provided me with the focus and motivation I needed. His self-discipline amazed me. He insisted we stick with our assignments until they were finished, and gently pulled me back on task each time I got distracted. However, once our work was completed, he was more than happy to linger and chat.

The more we talked, the more we found we had in common. We shared similar goals and values, and we both enjoyed music, dancing, sports, and spending time outdoors. We talked about the people we were dating, and about how nice it would be to feel as comfortable with them as we did with each other. I never considered that to be an omen, but perhaps it was.

When the term ended, I headed home, bidding farewell to Monte and to BYU. Though I expected to be on my way to the University of Idaho in ten short days, even the best-laid plans can suddenly change.

The day before I was to head back to the University of Idaho, I went to the temple with one of my former high school friends. He'd just returned from his mission, and although I had never been attracted to him before, I now had a little crush on him. We were both enrolled at the U of I, so we planned to make the 17 hour drive to northern Idaho together the next day.

I eagerly anticipated spending the whole day with him, but while we were in the temple, I received an undeniable prompting that I should return to BYU. It made no sense at all because when I had been admitted for summer term, the woman at the registration office had emphatically informed me that Fall registration was out of the question. She said their quota had already been far exceeded and there was absolutely no room for new students.

At the time I had just smiled and thought of the wonderful social life I would soon be returning to at the University of Idaho. "That's okay," I reassured her. "I'm only here for the Spanish credit. I have no intention of *ever* coming back to BYU."

In spite of what we had both said, I was registered within an hour of arriving back in Provo. Housing was also quickly taken care of because there happened to be a single vacancy in the house where I'd lived during the summer. God had told me to walk toward a closed door, and although it didn't seem logical to do it, when I obeyed Him, He had instantly flung the door wide open.

The first time I went to my new Spanish class, who should show up but my former study buddy. He was surprised and happy to see me, and we immediately reestablished our earlier study routine. However, from the beginning, I made it very clear that I wasn't interested in dating him. Although he had many impressive qualities, he simply did not match the description of the exciting guy I was looking for.

Even so, several weeks into the semester Monte asked if I would perhaps consider going on a double date with him just to help out his roommate, Kent. He explained that Kent was interested in dating my roommate, but he thought it would be best if their first date was a double. I'm still not sure whose idea the double date really was, but the four of us went to a concert and then to a dance at the student center. We had a good time, but I didn't expect to go out with Monte again because I was actively pursuing other interests, and *theoretically*, so was he.

About a month later, Monte called and asked if I might possibly be available to go with him to Homecoming. He quickly added that he knew he wasn't supposed to be asking, but he said Kent was on his way home from Hawaii with leis for each of his roommates to give to their Homecoming dates. They were also planning a fancy dinner at their apartment before the dance. He said he had already asked a couple of other girls, but he still hadn't been able to find anyone and he was hoping we could go just as friends.

What Monte didn't know was that the guy who had planned to be my Homecoming date had apologetically cancelled the day before because of an unexpected National Guard assignment. I was thrilled to have Monte rescue me from my disappointment, and happily agreed to go to the Neil Diamond Concert and the Homecoming Dance with him. However, I declined his invitation to the football game because I thought spending all that time together might give him the wrong idea. I still had absolutely no interest in a romantic relationship with him. Our study dates were working well, and I didn't want to complicate things.

Monte picked me up early for the concert and we spent a wonderful evening laughing, talking, and protecting our ears from the blasting volume. The next night was equally pleasant. He and his roommates served an impressive dinner, and then we went to the Homecoming Ball and danced the night away. But ever so wisely, Monte didn't ask me out again right away.

You could definitely say our relationship was not love at first sight, but somehow, over time, a little hint of romance found its way into our ongoing conversations. Monte patiently fanned that tiny spark while I continued to date other guys and suppress the recurring thought that he would be a significant part of my future.

The house I lived in happened to be located between Monte's apartment and the university, so in the afternoons or early evenings, Monte would frequently pop in unannounced. I welcomed the extra attention, or at least I did until I started dating an exciting new guy. He was a business major, and he matched my vision of Mr. Right better than anyone I had dated since my mission. Things seemed to be going well for us until Monte showed up a couple of times while my boyfriend was there. Even though I assured him Monte was just a study buddy, my boyfriend clearly wasn't happy about it.

To save my relationship, I decided I had to tell Monte to stop dropping in unannounced, so I asked him if he could come to my house the next evening to work on an assignment for our Spanish class. After we finished studying he got up to leave, and I followed him out onto my front porch. It was a cool November night, and by the time I gathered the courage to tell him, he was standing on the step below me with his arms around my waist. For some reason, my arms were draped across his shoulders. Maybe I was just trying to keep warm, who knows!

Anyway, as we stood eye to eye, I gently told Monte that even though I thought he was a super guy, and even though I really appreciated all he had done for me, and even though I enjoyed being with him, I needed him to quit coming to my house because it upset my boyfriend. Monte seemed totally understanding and assured me he would respect my wishes. Then a mischievous grin crossed his face and he offered to come over and tell my boyfriend he had nothing to worry about.

During the conversation, our faces had drawn closer and closer, and in an inexplicable moment, I leaned in and kissed him right on the mouth. To this day I'm not sure why that happened. I was just trying to let him down easy, not initiate our first kiss! Perhaps it shouldn't have been a surprise since we'd been standing there nose to nose for a while, but my behavior was so inconsistent with my words that it caught us both off guard.

Monte tells people it was the strangest experience of his life and the best kiss-off he ever had. He says he went home that night both elated and confused. But regardless, my purpose had been accomplished. Kiss or no kiss, we parted with the agreement that our contact would be limited to studying Spanish together on campus.

However, as luck—or destiny—would have it, my cool boyfriend and I broke up several weeks later. Though I felt the sting of rejection, I wasn't terribly upset because we obviously weren't a good match. As usual, I chatted with Monte about it after our next study date, and he kindly commiserated with me, confiding that things weren't going well for him in the dating department either.

A week or so went by, and then just two days before Christmas break, Monte called and asked if I'd like to go to dinner the next night. He said his friend, Lee, was coming into town and wanted to go on a double date. Since I was back to being unattached, I happily agreed to go.

Lee picked us up at my apartment and I quickly realized he was much more than just Monte's friend. He was also his great admirer. Throughout the dinner, he praised Monte repeatedly, expressing gratitude for things he had done for him, sharing stories of how Monte had profoundly influenced his life. He said he had joined the church a few years earlier because of Monte's example. Lee's stories and sincerity touched my heart and I felt like I was getting to know Monte in a whole new way.

After Lee dropped us off at my apartment, Monte lingered and we talked late into the night. Everything suddenly seemed so different. How could I have missed the obvious? He was definitely a diamond in the rough, and I was finally seeing the diamond whereas before I had only seen the rough. I went home for Christmas with stars in my eyes.

They say that absence makes the heart grow fonder, and while Monte and I were apart for those few weeks, my heart was ablaze with fondness. He was my new obsession, and I spent my vacation anxiously anticipating his phone calls. Long distance calls were expensive so he only called a few times, but when he did, he didn't seem concerned about the bill. We chatted at length about our relationship and wondered why things hadn't clicked for us before. I felt wonderfully in love and could hardly wait to be with him again.

However, when I got back to school, the stars that had glistened in my eyes during the break suddenly clouded over with fear. Was he really the one? I no longer felt confident that I'd found Mr. Right.

When we got together that first evening, I tried to discreetly backtrack, but Monte had no intention of losing the ground he had gained. He gently but firmly insisted it was time for us to date exclusively or not at all.

My mind went ballistic. Did I really want to burn all my bridges? What if I had just let my imagination run away with me while we were apart and this didn't work out after all? There were two other guys who had been quite flirtatious with me before the break, and I thought I should at least check them out before making a hasty decision. Monte listened patiently as I tried to tactfully explain my ambivalence. Finally, he interjected a few words of his own.

"Yes, I realize it is a calculated risk."

Perhaps he meant those words to be reassuring, but all I could think was, "You're right! You calculate, and I risk!" What did he have to lose? He was all in. I was the one who might be passing up the opportunity to meet the perfect guy.

But here was my dilemma. Even though I didn't feel madly in love anymore, I knew I didn't want Monte to walk out of my life. I also knew him well enough to know that unless I let go of all other romantic interests, he would be gone. Since I wasn't willing to let that happen, I apprehensively agreed. After all, I wasn't saying I would marry him. I was still free to change my mind any time I wanted to.

Even with my eating disorder and other symptoms of perfectionism secretly running rampant in my life, our relationship managed to progress, and Monte popped the question early in March. His proposal didn't catch me off-guard because our conversations had occasionally dipped into that pool of possibilities, but I wasn't yet ready to dive in. I still longed for that consistent spark of romantic excitement, and I also wanted desperately to overcome my eating disorder before I got married. I couldn't imagine telling Monte—or any other boyfriend—that I threw up every day.

My respect and admiration for Monte had definitely deepened over the past two months. We constantly shared our feelings and dreams with each other and had gradually become more and more a part of each other's lives. I knew he was a great guy, and the thought that I would someday marry him still lingered in the back of my mind, but it just wasn't enough. I needed that spark! Why did it have to be so elusive?

Unable to offer a more satisfying response to his proposal, I finally replied, "I'm not saying yes, but I'm not saying no." Then I hastily went on to explain that I loved him, but I was not in love with him, and that I needed to feel in love before I could say yes to anyone.

Nervous about his response, I was pleasantly surprised when I heard him say, "The train is in the station. You can jump on whenever you are ready."

At first, my delay tactic seemed to be working, but after another month of dating, it became painfully obvious that our relationship either needed to move forward or come to an end. We were edgy and unsettled with each other whenever we were together, but neither of us wanted to be apart. The thought of breaking up was unbearable, yet I still couldn't commit to marriage. I was so blinded by my perfectionism that I couldn't see how completely entangled I was in its tendrils of overwhelming fear and unrealistic expectations.

One day after a particularly edgy encounter, I blurted out to Monte, "Something has to change or this is never going to work!" When he asked what I thought needed to change, I admitted I had absolutely no idea.

He was planning to go home to Arizona that weekend, and I hoped the time apart would give us some clarity. Instead, while he was gone my thoughts took me on a journey of increasing distress and worry. What if Monte decided I wasn't worth all the hassle? What if his father told him to quit wasting his time with me? What if he met up with an old girlfriend and changed his mind about our relationship? By the time he called late Sunday night to see if he could come over, I was a wreck.

As soon as I opened the door, I could tell something was different. Instead of greeting me with a warm hug, he remained firmly planted in the doorway and asked if we could talk. Thinking he would follow me, I silently walked over to the couch where we always sat, but he went to a chair across the room. A feeling of panic washed over me. What was happening? After all his patient pursuing, was Monte going to call it quits?

Monte began by telling me he had spent the entire weekend trying to figure out exactly what needed to change in our relationship. He had read a lot, pondered a lot, and had discussed our situation with a former seminary teacher who had given him some definite insights. He said he believed couples should help each other accomplish their life goals, and that after thinking about it, he wasn't sure we would be good for each other over the long haul. "As a result," he said, "the train has left the station."

My mind struggled to understand exactly what that meant. Was this really the end? Had he actually decided he was through with me? Suddenly I felt sick to my stomach. Was there any chance the train might possibly return to the station?

Since he didn't seem in any hurry to clarify his intentions, I timidly ventured, "Do you think the train will ever come back?" Without hesitation, he responded, "It all depends on how things go from here."

Calmly and deliberately, then, Monte began to explain how things had to change before he would consider another proposal. In short, he called me on the carpet. Perfectionists tend to procrastinate, and I had honed my procrastination skills so well that I often had to stay up all night to get an assignment in on time. Monte knew I wanted to do well in school, and he realized that our time together had been distracting me from my homework. He said he would no longer contribute to my procrastinating by taking me out on dates. I would have to have my homework done in every class before he would take me anywhere, even if he had already purchased tickets for a movie, a concert, or some other event. He needed me to be more responsible if I was going to be his wife and the mother of his children.

Though that may sound demanding or chauvinistic to some, it was the exact boundary our relationship needed. Suddenly I was madly in love, anxious to prove I was the woman of his dreams.

During the next month, Monte followed through just as I knew he would. Only once did I try to persuade him to bend the rule since I knew I had plenty of time the next morning to get my homework done before class, but he would have none of it. We stayed home and I did my homework while he read a book. Under these new conditions our relationship flourished, and so did my grades. Five weeks later the train returned to the station.

This time when he asked me to marry him, my heart wanted to shout a joyous yes, but again I hesitated. Though things were now fantastic in our relationship, my eating disorder raged out of control, and Monte was still completely in the dark about it. I knew I couldn't hide it from him if we were married, nor did I want to. I firmly believed then—as I do today—that married couples who hide things from each other are headed for disaster. I had wanted so desperately to gain control so I could reveal my eating disorder only as a part of my past, but that was not my reality. The dreaded moment of truth had arrived, and I knew I must open my carefully guarded box of secrets and lay everything on the table.

The prospect terrified me. What were the chances that Monte would still want me once he was aware of all my shameful baggage? What if he rejected me? What would I do then? What would I say? I forced myself not to think about it. I was determined to be open and honest about absolutely everything before he decided if he still wanted me to answer that life-altering question.

First, I drew from the shadows all the sexual feelings and experiences that had caused me so much guilt and shame throughout the years. That seemed to be the safest place to start since sexual transgressions aren't uncommon, and I assumed they wouldn't be too shocking to him.

Monte's accepting words and loving reassurance gave me the courage to unveil the ugly details of my eating disorder. He listened intently to my long and tearful explanation of compulsion and misery. When I finished, he responded gently and with unconcerned optimism. He was confident this problem would be no match for everything he was learning in his upper division psychology classes about changing habits and addictions. He loved studying unorthodox solutions to difficult cases, and he seemed far more fascinated by my problem than worried about it. I was instantly infused with hope. Finally, someone was going to rescue me!

A few hours later we were on the phone with our parents, sharing the news of our engagement and checking calendars for the best possible dates. An August wedding would see us through summer school, give us adequate time to prepare, and avoid hazardous winter travel. And so it was agreed: August 16th in the Idaho Falls Temple.

Monte remained undaunted a week later when I hesitantly admitted my first relapse into my binge and purge cycle, but after several subsequent relapses, he called a truce. Without disclosing his mounting frustration, he calmly declared, "We're going to stop focusing on this until after we are married." That was all he said. He offered no further explanation.

Desperate to be in control before our wedding, I pleaded with Monte to reconsider, but he wouldn't be persuaded. He tenderly assured me he wasn't giving up; he just felt we needed to wait until we were married to deal with the problem. He never again asked me how I was doing with my battle, and he wouldn't allow me to tell him anything about it either. I continued to beg God to help me break free and gain at least some control, but the chains remained tightly in place.

My stress level soared. I was scheduled to start my fourth-grade teaching internship the week after our wedding and I didn't feel adequately prepared. I spent long hours doing lesson plans, finishing my regular class work, studying for finals, and getting ready for our wedding, but I still found time to throw up almost every time I ate anything.

Besides the fear of not being able to overcome my eating disorder, another fear haunted me. Over the years I had harbored a nagging anxiety about the marriage commitment. More than anything, I wanted that wonderful, unconditional love of a husband, but I couldn't imagine being forever certain I had chosen the right person. What if I married Monte but then another guy came along who would have clearly been a better match for me?

Thankfully that question was put to rest the week after I accepted Monte's proposal. We were sitting in church together when a very attractive guy walked in. I automatically began checking him out, wondering if he might be my type and if I might be able to capture his attention. Suddenly, in a tone of absolute conviction, distinct and forceful words came into my mind. "Hey! I don't do that anymore." It was an unexpected but important milestone in my life. My search was over.

As our courtship progressed, the certainty that I had found the right guy was repeatedly confirmed to me. Monte had a wonderful, anchoring influence in my life. He was as steady as I was erratic. He did everything he could to bring order to my chaotic life and calm my anxiety. We established a pattern of studying at the library every night, and he patiently tutored me in physics so I could complete the independent study course I had been procrastinating.

One day Monte showed up at my door with an article discussing the importance of sleep. He read to me about prisoners of war who were forced to stay awake for days to weaken their resistance. He hastily added that he wasn't trying to tell me what to do, but he said I might have more strength to deal with my challenges if I allowed myself to get more sleep. I knew he was right and I really wanted to change my nocturnal habits, but late at night was usually when my urge to binge and purge took on a life of its own.

About a month before our wedding, I took advantage of a long weekend and went home to work on my wedding dress with Mother. Getting the dress to fit properly was the usual ordeal. While Mother was adjusting and pinning the necessary alterations, she commented that Monte and I were a pair, since both of us had rather odd body shapes. I knew what she was talking about in my case because we had been over it a million times before, but I asked her what she meant about Monte. She named a couple of his body features, stating that standard patterns wouldn't fit him any better than they fit me. Immediately a new string of stressful thoughts marched through my mind. Our poor children! With two sets of weird genes to draw from, they didn't stand a chance!

Of course, Mother had no intention of hurting me or demeaning our bodies. She adored Monte, and she had made countless sacrifices over the years hoping to secure a measure of happiness for me. In her mind, it was a simple observation, but my perfectionism kept me playing the role of the unhappy victim until years later when I at last learned to love and let go.

After I finished my final exams, I hurried home again to help my mother with last-minute preparations. Monte wanted to come with me, but his classes weren't over yet so he had to stay in Provo. Once I was away from him, my fears kicked in with a vengeance. Would I really be able to be a good wife? What if I couldn't get over my eating disorder and he decided he didn't want me after all? I was so stressed I nearly drove myself crazy.

The night before the wedding, my dad came into my room. He told me he had been concerned about some of my choices throughout my dating years and was pleased that I was getting married in the temple to a good man. Then he said he wanted to share a few words of counsel with me.

In his gentle way, Daddy advised me to have faith as I began navigating the challenges of marriage and family life. He said I worried too much, and that I would be able to create the happy life I wanted for myself, for Monte, and for our unborn children if I would just learn to trust the Lord. His timely expression of love comforted me, as did the tender blessing he pronounced upon my head before I wearily crawled into bed. But the peaceful sleep I so desperately needed still didn't come.

Early the next morning, my family jumped into the car and began the eighty-minute drive to the temple where we were to meet Monte and his family. As usual, we were running late. Twenty minutes into the drive, Mother realized that my wedding dress was still hanging in the kitchen. Without the convenience of cell phones, the best we could do was race back home for it and hope Monte and his family would be patient and understanding.

When we finally reached the temple parking lot, Mother flung the door open before the car came to a stop. She ran in search of Monte and found him pacing the sidewalk in front of the temple. Apologizing repeatedly, she explained that our delay wasn't caused by cold feet, but by a forgotten bridal gown. Monte was obviously relieved, and he later admitted he had begun to wonder if I had succumbed to my fears and changed my mind.

Monte had never doubted his decision to marry me once we were engaged. Even on the eve of our wedding, he was blissfully calm. His brother, who shared a hotel room with him that night, told me he'd expected Monte to be antsy and stressed, or at least a little bit nervous. But he said Monte had gone to bed early and had slept like a baby.

Perhaps he wouldn't have slept so peacefully had he been able to see the storm clouds gathering just beyond the horizon.

# 10

# ONLY SUNSHINE FROM NOW ON . . . OR MAYBE NOT

*Marriage doesn't fix perfectionism*

August 16, 1972, will forever remain a landmark day in my life. Not only was this the day I set out on the grand adventure of marriage, it was also the day my eating disorder quietly slipped away. There was no heroic battle where I finally found the strength to overpower my fearsome dragon and thrust a dagger into its heart. It just seemed to vanish into thin air, almost as if it had never been a part of me.

My new husband initiated this long-awaited change as we drove home from the temple that Wednesday afternoon. His words were brief but compelling. "Sweetheart, I will always love you no matter how you look. I honestly don't care how fat you get. Just promise me that you will take responsibility for everything you put in your mouth. Please don't throw up anymore." It was a completely different approach, and in the glow of the moment, I promised I would do as he asked.

Our marriage brought a structured routine into my life, along with many new demands on my time and attention. Because my teaching job began right after we got back from our reception in Arizona, my days were immediately filled with the concerns of thirty-five fourth graders. I got home from school with barely enough time to fix dinner before Monte arrived.

After we ate, Monte sat at the kitchen table and did homework while I graded papers and prepared lesson plans. We went to bed early because he had to get up at three o'clock for his custodial shift. Our weekends were filled with laundry, grocery shopping, cleaning our tiny apartment, service projects, and inexpensive dates. I got pregnant during the first month of our marriage and I was soon dealing with exhaustion and morning sickness.

The many changes and new circumstances in my life created an environment that allowed my eating disorder to painlessly disappear. On the few occasions when I did sense old urges calling, a quiet voice in my head said, "I don't do that anymore," and my focus would shift elsewhere. It seemed my husband, my knight in shining armor, had truly rescued his damsel in distress.

When eating disorders became a topic of public interest years later, I wanted to help others who were struggling as I once had. Unfortunately, I didn't have a good understanding of all the factors that had created my change. Though I was living proof that it was possible to suddenly be free of a raging eating disorder, I knew there had to be more to it than a wedding ceremony. Many women with eating disorders were already married, so that obviously wasn't the solution for them.

From time to time I went to seminars or classes related to eating disorders, but they generally focused on the seriousness of the problem and what caused it, rather than on solutions. Though I found hints here and there, the pieces of this puzzle didn't really fall into place for me until many years later when I read a book titled *Change Anything: The New Science of Personal Success.*

Toward the end of the book, the authors explain that an addiction actually makes a physical change in a specific part of the brain. This change causes a behavior that began as something pleasant to turn into an urge, a craving, or a compulsion. The book discusses the importance of implementing multiple motivating influences to help the addict establish new patterns of behavior and give the brain time to readjust so it can begin to function normally again.

Finally everything made sense. Although my husband's support had been a critical factor in making the change I so desperately wanted, it certainly wasn't the only one. My teaching job required me to keep a strict daily routine which limited my access to food throughout most of the day. My bedtime immediately changed to accommodate Monte's early morning work schedule. My pregnancy soon began to make me so tired I could barely stay awake in the evening to grade my school papers. I planned and prepared healthy dinners and sat down at the table with Monte to eat them.

My focus changed from worrying about my eating disorder all the time to creating a comfortable home environment and helping students who struggled to progress in school. I also focused on preparing to bring a new little person into the world. All these factors, combined with Monte's wonderful support, opened the way for my eating disorder to quickly and quietly disappear.

But at the time of our marriage, I didn't recognize the importance of all the other changes going on in my life, so I gave Monte all the credit for ending my eating disorder. I praised his wonderful "arm of flesh," giving only minor lip service to Heavenly Father. Monte and I were both thrilled with my progress. Neither of us realized I was developing a dependency on him that would set us up for future conflict and pain.

Though food no longer dominated my existence, my perfectionistic fear of never being good enough lived on, attacking my happiness in many subtle ways. Sometimes I would try to quiet my insecurity by twisting Monte's words, forcing him to clarify their meaning and reassure me of his love and devotion. Or I would dispute his compliments regarding my skills or my appearance so he would adamantly disagree with my perception and assure me I was attractive and worthwhile. I wanted him to constantly reaffirm his love for me. No matter how many times I drank from the fountain of his love, my unquenchable thirst for self-worth was never satisfied for long.

Although I didn't understand what I was doing, it didn't take Monte long to figure it out. One day he stopped me midstream as I was once again distorting his words. "Elona," he said, "You need to believe I love you without dragging us through this conflict all the time. We only get to live each minute once, and then it's gone forever. I'd rather spend our time being happy instead of arguing. If you want to argue, you'll have to find someone else to argue with. I'm not playing this game anymore."

And he meant it. After that, he would listen to me when I poured out my insecurities, but he refused to respond when I twisted his words.

Though I could see the wisdom, I found no remedy for my insecurity, so my behavior persisted. In response, Monte brought home marriage enrichment books, inviting me to read and discuss them with him. He expressed his love for me multiple times a day, but whenever I slipped into manipulation mode, he would disengage. Although it sometimes made me angry or frustrated, his steadiness increased my confidence and trust in him.

One evening, several months into our marriage, I faced an unexpected moment of truth. Monte had gone to a study group, and I was home feeling stressed because I was behind in grading my school papers. A cake I'd made earlier in the week beckoned to me, offering to relieve my stress. Answering the call seemed harmless enough because I hadn't had any problem with my eating disorder since our marriage . . . until one slice of cake turned into two, and then two became three. Soon I had eaten far more cake than I had ever intended, and I began chiding myself for my lack of control.

As I drank a large glass of milk to balance out all the sugar, I kept telling myself everything was okay, but when I finished drinking the milk, my stomach felt way too full and the old familiar lies began stealing into my mind. "You've done so well. It wouldn't be a big deal to throw up just this once. You'll feel sick all night if you don't. You don't have to tell Monte, because you won't ever let this happen again."

Then another persuasive thought chimed in. "You really do need to throw up because all that sugar will be bad for the baby." I sensed the danger in those thoughts, but I brushed the warning aside. I needed to believe the lies to justify what I had already decided to do.

Although I dreaded making myself throw up again, I moved forward as if I had no choice. Monte would soon be home, and I had to hurry because I didn't want him to know I'd chosen to break my promise. Then another lie came to soothe my growing guilt: in the future, I would keep *all* sweets out of the house so I could never be tempted like this again. Once I believed I had a redeeming plan in place, throwing up "one last time" didn't seem so bad.

With the conflict seemingly resolved, I quickly went into the bathroom, but as I lifted the toilet seat and stared into that familiar abyss, I began to waver. I desperately wanted to keep my promise to Monte. He trusted me, and I hated the thought of deceiving him. I had told him every one of my dark secrets before we got married. Did I really want to have another secret to hide? I loved the amazing sense of freedom I had experienced over the last several months. What if I couldn't make myself quit after starting again? Maybe this was not such a good idea after all. I left the bathroom and sat down on the edge of our bed to further ponder my situation.

I had a serious dilemma on my hands. My stomach was bulging, and I knew what the consequences would be if I didn't follow through and throw up. I'd feel miserable all night, I wouldn't get much sleep, and I'd be exhausted at school the next day. Within a few hours, foul burps would start, and they would probably take days to go away.

There was no question. It had to be done. I took my new determination back into the bathroom, but after another moment of deliberation, I walked out again. I went into the kitchen, wiped down the counter, straightened the towels, and returned to the bathroom. What was I going to do? I was completely torn.

Back and forth I went for almost an hour before I heard Monte coming up the walk. Panic seized me. Now I would really have to be sneaky. My mind quickly reviewed all my old strategies for hiding the evidence. I would run the water in the sink to muffle the sounds of my throwing up. I would flush instantly after throwing up to prevent any lingering odor in the bathroom. I would use our minty toothpaste to cover my breath. It still wasn't too late!

But I continued to vacillate. Here was the person who had finally opened the door to the freedom I had so desperately longed for. Did I really want to deceive him? Was I ready to risk all the progress of the last several months just to get rid of an overdose of cake, a glass of milk, and some water?

Suddenly reason returned! The debate was over.

I wearily greeted Monte, changed into my nightgown, and brushed my teeth. I was finally ready to pay the inevitable price for not emptying my stomach. It would be a very long and uncomfortable night as my stomach did its best to cope. The discomfort would most likely carry into the next day. The nasty burps would certainly linger. I might even gain an extra pound or two. My mind relaxed as I realized I could live with each of those consequences, even though I knew I wouldn't like them.

After kneeling for our nightly prayer, I gingerly positioned myself on my side of the bed. Monte said his own prayer and then hopped into bed beside me. Just that little jostling of the bed made my stomach hurt, but I knew there was no point in trying to find a more comfortable position. Time was now the only cure. Monte snuggled toward me and wrapped his arm around me as he always did. The pressure made me feel like I was going to explode. "Please don't touch me," I groaned.

"What's the matter?" he asked in a concerned tone as he quickly withdrew his arm. "Is something wrong with the baby?"

"No, everything's fine with the baby," I mumbled.

"Then what's wrong?"

I wanted to think of a good way to answer, but the words just came tumbling out. "Oh, Honey," I wailed. "I was so stupid! While you were gone I ate too much cake. I decided I needed to throw it all up, so I drank a bunch of water, but then I just couldn't bring myself to do it. So now I feel totally bloated and sick."

He instantly sprang to his knees and leaned over me. His reaction startled me, and for a split second, I thought he was angry. But then he began showering my face with kisses as he jubilantly repeated, "I love you! I love you! I love you!" Although I didn't feel like much of a conqueror, Monte knew how to celebrate the victory!

We stayed awake and talked for a long time that night. After I explained all the consequences I would be facing, we went on to talk about our gratitude for each other and about our hopes and dreams for the new little person coming into our lives. We talked about Monte's upcoming graduation, and about things we planned to do to help some of my more difficult fourth-grade students. We talked about what the future might hold for us and the joy of sharing it with each other. When we finally turned out the light, my heart was even fuller than my stomach.

The inevitable consequences came throughout the night and lingered on into the next few days just as I had known they would, but they were soon forgotten. However, I will never forget that night. It was another significant landmark in my life. Though I had faced the enemy with a vastly wavering resolve, in the end, I had prevailed. However, because of my husband's role in that battle, my confidence in his ability to fix my problems was reinforced. I had much to learn about trusting in any arm of flesh—no matter how wonderful—but I didn't yet have the experience and understanding I needed to embrace the truth.

Our simple daily routines continued, and the following spring, just three days after I finished teaching school, I gave birth to a beautiful baby boy. After much discussion, we named him David. Once I got past the nightmare of postpartum blues, David enriched and delighted my life in endless ways.

My vision of the perfect family was unfolding right before my very eyes. I had an awesome husband who took care of my needs, an amazing little son who gave our lives purpose and joy, and even though I was eating generous meals and snacks every day, my body was quickly stabilizing at a comfortable weight. I seemed to be on a direct path to the life I had always dreamed of. As I gazed happily at the sunrise, I was oblivious to the heavy clouds rolling in behind me.

# 11

# SURPRISE STORMS
# ON THE HORIZON

*New babies and good jobs don't fix perfectionism*

Several months before David was born, Monte was accepted into a doctoral program. We had a goal of finishing school without any debt, but his doctoral program didn't allow students to have jobs because of their demanding coursework. We wondered if I should apply for a teaching job, but neither of us wanted to leave our baby with a sitter every day.

When we learned there were openings for head residents in the girls' dorms on campus, we eagerly applied. The job seemed like the perfect solution since it provided housing along with a small salary. Although most of the responsibility would fall on me, I would only need to get a babysitter once a week for staff meetings. During our interview, we were told our application looked impressive, but the competition was stiff since over fifty couples had applied for the two openings.

Weeks passed and finally, a letter came from the housing office. With pounding heart, I began reading its contents to Monte. The letter praised our outstanding qualifications, but it also said that two other couples had been selected to fill the positions. My disappointment quickly turned to anger as my perfectionistic thoughts magnified the sting of our rejection.

Even though the next paragraph explained that our application would be kept on file as second alternates, I crumpled the letter and tossed it into the garbage.

Monte watched my reaction in surprise and quickly retrieved the letter. He saw no rejection in the letter at all, but only exciting possibilities. He reread the part about being selected as alternates and reminded me that it was not so bad to come in fourth out of that many applicants. His logical mind focused on several points that my emotional reaction had caused me to miss. The job didn't start until August, and it was currently only April. Students' lives are particularly susceptible to unexpected change, so alternates have a good chance of ending up with the job.

Eventually I agreed that his wait-and-see approach was probably better than my idea of sending the housing office a spicy letter of mutual rejection. Less than a month later we received a letter offering us the job. We would be moving into the dorms in mid-August.

Meanwhile, I needed to finish two summer classes to complete my graduation requirements. Six weeks of classwork didn't seem like a big deal, but juggling school and a baby proved to be more challenging than it looked on paper. I was still riding the wave of postpartum blues, and I had a husband who knew nothing about child care.

Each time I went to class, I left the baby fed, dry, and usually asleep. However, the baby didn't always stay asleep, which made Monte very nervous because he wasn't at all comfortable changing diapers. On one occasion, he barely made it through the ordeal of a major blow out. Still, we all managed to survive, and a few days before our first anniversary, Monte and I donned caps and gowns and officially received our diplomas. One of my favorite pictures is of the two of us in graduation garb holding our chubby little three-month-old son between us.

A few days after graduation we moved into the tiny head resident apartment in Snow Hall and began a new routine. We were responsible for 120 girls, most of them fresh out of high school. They often stopped by our apartment to share their ups and downs about school, roommates, family, friends, and boyfriends. A couple of girls offered to watch David whenever we needed a babysitter, and sometimes they would come by our apartment just to play with him. He was a ready cure for homesickness, boyfriend blues, and test anxiety.

I loved the steady flow of activity in the dorm, as well as the opportunity to share my "wisdom" and experience as a married woman and a new mother. Of course, the job had its downside too. Sometimes I had to deal with girls who didn't do their cleaning assignments, or who took their roommates' food, or who tried to sneak in after curfew. But the joy of sharing in their lives far outweighed the problems.

As much as I loved working with the girls, there were other aspects of my job that I didn't follow through on very well. Turning in maintenance requests wasn't difficult, but I was also supposed to do cleaning checks of each apartment every Saturday, and I often let that task slide. The girls generally didn't mind, but when I went to my weekly meetings and all the other head residents seemed to be performing perfectly, I felt guilty and inadequate. I knew my supervisors would be disappointed in me if they discovered I wasn't doing everything they expected. Each week I went home promising to be more worthy of their praise, but I continued to fall short.

My life was wonderful in so many ways, but my underlying insecurities surfaced frequently. I didn't yet understand my perfectionism nor did I have tools to deal with it in a healthy way, so my unchecked thoughts would often run wild. "What if people find out I'm not as good as they think I am? What if Monte gets tired of me? What if something happens to him and I lose his anchoring influence in my life? What if something happened to my precious baby?"

David meant everything to me, and I constantly worried that I wouldn't be a good enough mother for him as he grew up. And there was always that overarching, haunting question, "What if I never become good enough to make it to the Celestial Kingdom with my treasured little family?"

Thankfully those thoughts didn't dominate my life like my eating disorder had. The structure Monte maintained in his life brought a huge measure of peace and order to mine. David delighted us anew every single day. Watching him grow and develop through each stage of babyhood filled our world with wonder. David adored Monte, and Monte adored David. The girls in the dorms showered him with attention and fun little gifts. His first steps were joyously celebrated throughout the whole building.

Not long after we started our head resident job, Monte's mother was diagnosed with cancer. She longed to spend time with David since he was her first grandchild, but we lived twelve hours away. We couldn't visit her very often because of school and work, and she couldn't visit us very often because of her chemo treatments.

During one of her rare trips to Provo, she offered to do some mending for me. Instead of appreciating her thoughtfulness, I interpreted her offer to mean she thought I was an incompetent homemaker. Although life is sweeter when we assume everyone has positive intentions, perfectionism doesn't leave room for that loving approach. I finally gave her a couple of David's little shirts to mend, but sadly, whenever I noticed her handiwork as I dressed him, I felt guilty instead of grateful.

My negative attitude toward my body had diminished to some degree, but it still tripped me up regularly. During my pregnancy, I struggled with feeling fat, and therefore, automatically ugly. I hated the growing stretch marks that crept up my stomach the last few months before David's delivery. After he was born, my stomach looked like a soggy, oversized waffle. If I was in a good mood, Monte could pat it as I lay on the bed and we would laugh as it quivered like Santa's proverbial "bowl full of jelly." But when I was in a bad mood, I found no humor as I miserably imagined how awful I would look after having our other babies.

Monte excelled in graduate school and was chosen to implement a literacy program in Guatemala the following summer. This opportunity fit perfectly with our head residency job because the dorms were vacant during the summer term. Monte's professors were excited that we both spoke Spanish, and I was excited to go, but once we got to Guatemala and I grasped the task before us, I kept wondering if we were doing enough. We adored the people we worked with, and everyone adored David, but there was no way to accomplish all that needed to be done in just two short months. Establishing a solid foundation for the program became our main focus. We worked hard, and when it was time to go we left the program in the hands of some wonderful people we had trained.

At the end of August, we were back in the dorms with a new group of girls. Once again we enjoyed getting to know each of them and their unique personalities, but another pregnancy was soon draining my energy. It brought with it the expected waves of morning sickness, but this time they would often linger throughout the entire day.

During my pregnancy, a new worry began to invade my mind. David had awakened a special kind of love and affection within me. He was the light of my life and the joy of my existence. I felt certain I could never love another child as much as I loved him. This poor new baby! I would have to *pretend* I loved him or her as much as I loved David.

Dorm parenting continued to bring a mixture of guilt and pleasure. I never did get those cleaning checks down to a strict, weekly routine, but we maintained order and developed wonderful, enduring friendships with many of the girls. The school year ended in a whirlwind of cleaning checks and fond farewells. The baby was due the following week, and we were scheduled to move to Portland, Oregon for Monte's summer internship a few weeks later.

While awaiting the pains that would signal the imminent birth, I cleaned, packed, and tried to keep David entertained. He couldn't understand why all his "big sisters" had suddenly vanished. Life was about to undergo a huge change for all of us.

Almost a week after my due date, I delivered our second son. Fortunately, I didn't have postpartum depression this time, and I was wonderfully surprised to discover that my ability to love had magically expanded. I didn't have to pretend to love this baby after all. He immediately commanded my whole heart just as David did, although that didn't seem logical or even possible. But it was true. I had done all that worrying for nothing.

Three weeks after his arrival, we stuffed our little car to overflowing with babies and belongings and headed north for our next adventure. It was another new beginning and I eagerly turned my back on all past storm clouds, anticipating a fresh new start under Portland's summer sunshine.

# 12

# STORMY SKIES IN PORTLAND

*A marriage crisis*

The first thing we did when we drove into town that Friday afternoon was purchase a newspaper. We needed to find a place to live immediately since Monte's job started on Monday. We were definitely blessed with several small miracles that weekend. Even without the convenience of the internet, in less than two hours we had signed a contract for a two bedroom apartment in a nice, suburban area.

Since there weren't many members of our church in the area, we were thrilled to be greeted by two other young Latter-day Saint families who lived in the same apartment complex. They welcomed us warmly and spread the word that we were in town. By nightfall, our unfurnished apartment had a foam pad for our bed, a card table for us to eat on, and four folding chairs, all compliments of generous people in our new ward family. By Tuesday other members had provided us with a crib and an old couch. A few weeks later, we were given a real bed and a few other items of furniture. Clearly, God was watching over us, inspiring others to be His hands in caring for our needs.

Meanwhile, Monte's new schedule was extremely demanding. He was gone during most of our waking hours except on

Sundays. We knew at the outset that it would be a challenging summer, but we figured since it was only a three-month internship we could manage it. I had imagined myself as the perfect, supportive wife who did it all without complaint. However, my good intentions were no match for my new reality. Being on my own every day with a toddler and a newborn in a new area was more difficult than I anticipated. My hormones still weren't back to normal, and when it came right down to it, I was an emotional wreck.

My friendship with Shirley Ryan became my lifeline. She lived in the complex, and like me, she had two small children. Her husband was studying for the bar exam and was hardly ever around, so our situations were quite similar. Shirley was creative and much more on top of things than I was so I frequently felt inferior to her, but I loved spending time with her and she obviously valued our friendship. She initiated play dates, called to chat when the kids were napping, and even invited us on an occasional afternoon trip to visit her parents. Sometimes we fed our kids dinner together since our husbands both came home late. I don't know how I would have made it through that summer without her.

Still, I continued to struggle with feelings of inadequacy. Thoughts that I should be doing a better job as a wife and mother and daughter and sister and church member constantly plagued me. And to top it all off, a few weeks into the summer, Monte read a book which persuaded him that we would be more healthy, happy and clear-headed if we made a radical change in our diet.

Being healthier sounded good to me, but the details of the diet sounded totally foreboding. There would be no sugar, no dairy, no white flour, and no meat. Even more challenging, we couldn't combine fruits with other foods. If we wanted to have an apple or a banana or an orange as part of our meal, we had to eat it first and then wait half an hour before eating anything else. It sounded impossible to me, but Monte was so excited about it I felt compelled to try. Otherwise, I would be an unsupportive wife, and that was simply not acceptable.

The experience turned out to be horrible for me! The altered eating schedule and unusual menus were overwhelming. I already struggled just to get to the grocery store because the streets were unfamiliar, and they wound through trees, adjoining neighborhoods and a business district. Every time I went out, I was afraid I would get lost with my babies and not be able to find my way home.

Shopping with two kids is rarely a good idea, but if you don't know the store, it is an extremely bad idea. I didn't know where to look for anything I needed, so by the time I was half way through my grocery list, the baby would be fussing, and David would be endlessly trying to crawl out of the cart. It was every mother's nightmare!

Much of the time I felt like a caged animal, and my response was to sneak a treat. I felt guilty whenever I cheated on the diet because I knew Monte was counting on me. How could I be so disgustingly weak and deceptive? Of course, Monte, true to his nature, was disciplined and positive, confident that we would soon be thinking more clearly and feeling wonderfully invigorated.

I made it through the awkwardness of declining the yummy looking treats Shirley brought over, but a church dinner proved to be the last straw. Not a single thing on the menu worked with our food plan, so we just sat there with empty plates. When the people next to us asked why we weren't eating, I stumbled over my words trying to find an answer that didn't seem too weird. Suddenly it was evident to me that if our family adopted this diet, we would quickly become "freaks of society." How could I inflict that stigma on our precious children—or on myself, for that matter—regardless of how healthy we became?

Several days later, after repeatedly envisioning the isolated course our lives would take if we continued to eat this way, I felt I had struck on the only possible solution. Monte needed a different wife. He needed someone who would support him better than I could. My heart ached as I considered the possibility of dissolving our marriage, but my perfectionistic thinking left no space for any other option. A few nights later, after serving our unconventional dinner, I tearfully told Monte we needed to get a divorce.

Once he got past the initial shock, Monte tried to put his arms around me and reassure me of his love, but I adamantly resisted. If our marriage had to end, I didn't want to complicate things by melting into his embrace. My rejection must have been painful to him, but he responded calmly, asking if it would be okay to wait until Sunday to discuss my feelings. He said he needed some time to think about what I had told him, and he also wanted to talk about it when we weren't so tired.

A few tense days passed, and when Sunday afternoon arrived we sat down across the kitchen table from each other since I still wasn't allowing Monte to touch me. He first expressed his complete devotion to our family, and gently chided me for thinking he might ever consider exchanging his wife and children for a healthier diet. He then apologized for the overwhelming stress he had caused me, and acknowledged that he had been unwise to initiate such a big change when our lives were already engaged in so many transitions.

Throughout the following weeks, Monte made a special effort to be attentive to my needs. He even managed to get his boss to give him a day off so we could go to the beach with Shirley and her husband. We had a marvelous time wading in the chilly waves and eating crab salad at a quaint little restaurant. That excursion is one of my favorite memories of our stay in Portland.

If I were faced with a similar situation today, I think I would just raise my eyebrows at Monte and laugh. Then I'd probably say something like, "Wow, Honey! That might be a good experiment for us to try someday, but my world is way too unstable to throw in such a drastic change right now. If you would like me to pick up some different snacks for you to eat while you're at work, I'd be happy to do that."

I've changed a lot since then, but at the time, I wanted to please him so much that I didn't even think about honoring my own needs. I had simply gone along with it, hoping I could somehow measure up.

At the end of the summer, we again piled babies and belongings into the car, promising to stay in touch with our wonderful Portland friends. This time we drove to Madison, Wisconsin where Monte would spend a semester studying statistics at the local university.

We instantly fell in love with our cute little student apartment, the beautiful nearby lake, the amazing fall colors, and the diversity of our neighbors. Despite my insecurities, I quickly reached out to those around us, and we established many new friendships in the apartment complex as well as in our church group. Almost everyone was a long way from home, and it was comforting to connect and depend on each other.

Our new friends included people from all across the United States as well as couples from Israel and China. I loved hearing about their lives and their travel experiences, but the more I listened, the more my perfectionism invited me to see myself as a dumb little nobody from nowhere. I was most uncomfortable when the conversation turned to politics because I didn't listen to the news so I had no opinion or insights about national and world issues.

But I'm a people person, and I repeatedly found myself enthralled by the individuals we interacted with. The semester ended way too soon for me, and again we bid our fond farewells to people we had come to love in just a few short months. This time we turned our faces westward and set out on the long, wintry drive back to BYU where Monte would finish his degree.

It was another new beginning, and I excitedly anticipated leaving all the shadows of fear and insecurity behind me and settling into the perfect life. I had everything I'd dreamed of—a wonderful husband, two healthy, adorable children, a cozy little home, and more than enough money from Monte's internship to cover our bills. Of course, I knew there would be challenges, since challenges are an inevitable part of life, but I was confident I would soon be the exemplary wife and mother I had failed to be in the past. I happily rejoiced in the vision of a bright and cloudless future.

# 13

# LINGERING CLOUDS OVER FIX-IT MOM

*The joy and pain of parenting*

Our home was in an older neighborhood in South Provo. Although interior design is not my strength, I threw myself into painting walls, sewing curtains, and finding gently used furniture for each room. When spring came, I attacked the overgrowth in our backyard with a vengeance, envisioning our children happily playing there for many years to come.

In spite of energetic efforts and my overwhelming love for my family, this new adventure was again overshadowed by the thought that I was not yet "good enough." Although I established lovely friendships with many of the other young mothers in the ward, I immediately felt they were all better than I was at managing their children, sharing their talents, and following the counsel of church leaders. And no matter what I did to improve, my perfectionism would only allow me to focus on my imperfections.

We quickly became close friends with Hans and Uta Henchen, a delightful German couple who lived across the street from us. Our lives blended easily because the Henchen's had two small children, and like Monte, Hans was a student at BYU. Uta and I often arranged to help each other with our daily tasks, or take the kids to the park, or go grocery shopping together. For a while, their family came over to our house for dinner at least twice a week.

Once when I took my kids to Idaho to visit my parents, Uta and her children came with us. The kids were enchanted by the animals and had a wonderful time climbing on tractors, gathering eggs, and "helping" my dad milk the cows. Uta marveled at Mother's bountiful gardens overflowing with fruits, vegetables, and beautiful flowers.

Sadly, my insecurities tainted those few days that might otherwise have been filled with pure delight. I felt jealous and irritable when I noticed my mother fussing profusely over Uta's children while paying little attention to mine. Though I tried to hide my feelings, I wasn't entirely successful. By the time we got home, I had created a strain on our friendship that took months to repair.

My need to be—or at least appear to be—the perfect family created stress at every turn. It caused me to be critical of my husband and children when I could have been enjoying them and rejoicing in the abundant goodness in our lives. In my heart I treasured my family more than life itself, but the flow of love in our home was often interrupted by my outbursts of frustration as I tried to make everyone conform to my expectations, and to my understanding of God's expectations. While I diligently reached out to encourage and support people outside of our home, I unconsciously did the exact opposite to those who meant the most to me.

When I got pregnant with our third child, we decided our little house wouldn't be adequate for the eight children we planned to have. We shopped around and soon purchased a lot in the nearby town of Orem. After word got around the ward that we were building a new house, an older lady bluntly informed me that I was being ungrateful and extravagant because she had raised eight children in a home with the exact same floor plan as mine.

Since I worried about everyone's opinion, I readily shouldered this new load of guilt, fearful that God might view our move as unnecessary and prideful. Of course, Monte took a far more healthy approach. When I told him what she had said, he just laughed and reminded me that where and how we lived was none of her business.

On March 7, 1977, we moved into our new home. We became part of a quickly developing, modest neighborhood, which meant we were instantly surrounded by a lot of young families. Most of them were active members of our faith so our lives quickly became intertwined. Our children found tons of new friends to play with, and I found many young mothers to compare myself with. Though I enjoyed pleasant friendships with everyone I met in our new area, I usually kept a critical eye out, constantly comparing, constantly judging, constantly seeking to mask my many imperfections.

Before Monte and I celebrated our tenth anniversary, our family included all of our six children—four sons and two daughters. I guess eight was a little too ambitious for us! Each child brought their own unique joy and wonder to our family. I was amazed to find that my heart magically expanded with each birth, and I adored each one of them just as I had adored David when he was our only child.

We wanted to give our children every opportunity to become extraordinary people. Through the years we invited foreign exchange students and others to live with us so our children would appreciate people from other cultures. I arranged for them to sing for the elderly in care centers or in their homes so they would be comfortable with people who were ill or aging. I enrolled them in weekly music lessons and signed them up for all kinds of sports. We required them to do their homework and family chores before playing after school.

As our children experienced their own growing pains, I agonized right along with them. I desperately wanted them to be happy, and often tried to "fix things" for them. I thought if I were a really good mother, I would always know what to say and how to make everything work out right for them. When David got a B in his drafting class, I felt he deserved an A. He had worked hard in that class but some extenuating circumstances had prevented him from finishing the last touches on his final project. I went to his teacher and asked him to give David a little more time. He was extremely reluctant, but I persisted until he gave in and David got the A.

When things didn't go the way I thought they should, I turned to my problem-solving husband. He tried to be patient with my frustrations and encouraged me to remember that our children were still learning. After these intense conversations, he often brought home a new parenting book for us to read together. Although I prayed for help with my struggles, in reality, I had far more confidence in Monte's ability to solve my problems and affirm my self-worth than I did in God's willingness to help me.

When we built our new home, I happily agreed to put Monte's office in the farthest, quietest corner of the basement. There he could read, ponder, and study to his heart's content without being interrupted by whatever else was going on in our home. It had seemed like such a good idea at the time, but as our kids got older and parenting became more and more stressful, Monte would retreat to his study and remain blissfully oblivious to the chaos going on in my world.

Occasionally, when I became totally distraught with our children, I'd stomp downstairs and interrupt his peace. "Monte, I've had it!" I'd storm. "If you don't come up and make these kids obey, I'm leaving and *you* can get dinner on the table!"

In that worked-up state, if Monte didn't respond immediately— and in a manner that soothed my distress—I would blurt out all sorts of accusations. Though I hated myself for attacking him, once I got started I couldn't seem to stop. Unfortunately for everyone involved, I hadn't yet developed the tools I needed to manage my stress in a constructive way.

Usually Monte stepped in calmly and the kids got the message that it was time to conform to my demands, but sometimes he resorted to anger too. When his harsh words sent the children fearfully scurrying to comply, it *really* upset me. They already had one angry parent after them. They obviously did not need another. I wanted Monte to be patient and loving as he applied his more effective coercion tactics. The poor guy! He couldn't win. Even though he was doing his best to support me, he still caught the brunt of my criticism and judgment.

Sundays were especially difficult. It was one thing to fail in the privacy of my own home, but at church my failings were on display for all to see. Our children's rowdy behavior in sacrament meeting drove me crazy. I took treats and coloring books and crayons and picture books to keep them silently occupied, but nothing worked. One year I spent months making clever little "quiet books" with things to touch, tie, twist, match, and snap. Those helped for about a week . . . until the kids started fighting over who got to play with them first.

My disapproving looks and whispered threats yielded only minor impact on their behavior. Sometimes I made them sit quietly on the couch after we got home so they could "practice" what they were supposed to be doing during church meetings. What foolish torment I inflicted on myself and my family in the name of God and the Celestial Kingdom, when in reality I was frantically trying to appease my need to look good in the eyes of other people.

Sometimes I thought myself into such a frenzy that I would tell Monte he was in charge of the kids after church. I would drive off, wishing I could run away and never again have to deal with the pain I was feeling. Of course, after crying my eyes out, or screaming at God, or both, I always realized that everything I really cared about was right back there in my home. I didn't want to do anything that would hurt my family. I just wanted the pain to stop. It was that same agonizing pain I had lived with during my eating disorder, only now I had precious little ones depending on me, and I desperately feared I would never be good enough to get them all back to the Celestial Kingdom.

On these occasions I would usually find a place to park and try to read my scriptures. Most often I fell asleep and woke up sometime later with a more hopeful perspective. Then I'd write some new goals and design a new job chart. Before returning home I'd always promise myself and God that I would be better in the future, and for a while I would be a softer, kinder wife and mother. But eventually I would slip back into my familiar patterns of frustration and coercion.

The intense feelings of worthlessness which I had so thoroughly cultivated during my eating disorder returned regularly, raising questions that hastened my downward spiral. Wouldn't my children be better off without me? If I were gone, wouldn't Monte find another wife who would be a more positive influence on our children?

Still, I didn't believe Monte's new and improved wife would ever be able to *love* my precious children as much as I did. They meant absolutely everything to me. Why was it so impossible for me to translate my love into the "firm yet gentle" parenting I envisioned?

Throughout the years I kept thinking I should be doing daily scripture study. I had repeatedly been taught that a daily dose of scripture study would increase my spirituality and make it easier to cope with the stresses in my life. Monte was the perfect example of a dedicated student of the scriptures. It was a trait I admired in him even before we started dating. He continually impressed me with his consistency and his insights. How I wished I could be more like him!

I envied people at church who talked about the guidance they received from scripture study, and I viciously condemned myself for not being spiritual enough to make it a daily practice. I made many attempts, and I did enjoy a few sweet experiences with the scriptures, but sooner or later—usually sooner than later—my best resolves to make scripture study a permanent routine in my life fell by the wayside.

While I couldn't seem to get into the scriptures, I eagerly delved into the childrearing books Monte brought home, reading their stories and advice with great interest. Monte was glad to see me studying those books, but he periodically commented that I would get better results if I combined my study of those books with a study of the scriptures. Of course I knew he was right, but I just couldn't make it happen. It became one more thing for me to feel guilty about.

Although I never felt adequate in my parenting, our children enriched, delighted, and gave purpose to my life. We worked and played and laughed together. Countless treasured moments are recorded on the pages of our family photo albums. We traveled to visit friends and relatives, we attended yearly family reunions in the mountains or on the beach, and one Christmas we took a wonderful trip to Disneyland, Sea World, and Tijuana.

But even with so much goodness in my life, the fundamental, constant sense of peace and happiness I sought always remained out of reach. Just as I had felt that I couldn't be happy unless I was the best reader in the second grade or the skinniest girl in high school, I now felt that I couldn't be happy unless I was the best mother, wife, homemaker, and church member around. The voice in my head kept promising me I would find happiness if I could just become more organized, more spiritual, more in control. Trapped in my fears and perfectionism, I not only invited storm clouds to follow me, but I actually created them.

# 14

# A PILL TO CHASE
# THE CLOUDS AWAY?

*Exploring medication and other remedies for depression*

Depression became a regular visitor, and I found myself wanting to sleep the days away just to avoid my thoughts and the stress they brought with them. But I had young children, so I forced myself to get out of bed and endure a minimum daily routine. Whenever I had to go out, I always managed to put on a happy face. I cried myself to sleep every night, but I did my best to hide my tears from the kids. Monte became deeply concerned and finally persuaded me to consult with our family doctor. However, I made it very clear that regardless of what the doctor said, I would not be taking any medication.

During the usual long wait at the doctor's office, I began wondering what I was going to say to explain my situation. My mind reflected on earlier visits when my doctor had lavishly praised me for being strong, capable, and uncomplaining. As I imagined telling him that I now cried all the time and spent every possible moment in bed, my pride recoiled and tears of humiliation began to trickle down my cheeks.

Those negative thoughts quickly multiplied, cycling repeatedly through my head. Though embarrassed by my tears, the more I tried to stop, the more I wept. Since cell phones were still a thing of the future, I eventually composed myself enough to ask the receptionist if I could use her phone to call my husband. As soon as I heard his voice, I totally fell apart. Between sobs, I told him I couldn't do it and I was going home. He pleaded with me to stay a little longer and within ten minutes he was sitting beside me in the waiting room.

His presence was wonderfully comforting, but as soon as the nurse called my name and showed us to an examination room, my tears started again. By the time the doctor came in fifteen minutes later, I was blubbering incoherently. Monte briefly explained how I had been acting for the past several months, and the doctor immediately began trying to convince me that depression medication was the solution to my problem. Of course, I shook my head and stubbornly resisted. Finally, after much testing of my doctor's patience, I agreed to at least *purchase* the prescription so I would have it on hand, even if I never used it.

Monte went with me to the pharmacy to pick up the prescription and then to get some lunch. I was so exhausted I could barely eat, and when I got home I collapsed on my bed. Instead of going to sleep, I laid there staring at the tiny prescription bottle in my hand. After a while, I focused my eyes and began to read the warnings on the label. Suddenly new waves of anxiety were sweeping over me.

Once again, I called my rescue-man husband. This time he begged me to put my fears on hold for a few hours and take a nap. There was no internet for him to consult, but he promised he would go to the university library and copy the complete report on this particular medication from the pharmaceutical books so we could look at it together.

That night, we scrutinized the tedious pages that explained all the possible side effects in graphic detail. We found everything from severe drowsiness, to itching, to a variety of ticks, to heart problems, to kidney failure, and even sudden death. The list went on and on and on! My nap must have worked its magic because rather than becoming more fearful, I was amused by the images that came to my mind. The risks of "the cure" seemed so much worse than dealing with the depression. Suddenly, I began pantomiming each symptom.

Monte watched in cautious amazement. After he felt sure I hadn't lost my mind, he playfully joined in my silliness, adding his own creative interpretations. Soon we were laughing hysterically. Before we went to bed that night, the little white pills were declared deadly, or at least undeniably toxic, and we ceremoniously stashed them in the back of the medicine cabinet.

Throughout the ensuing weeks, when I felt dark or tearful I would wonder if it was time to take one of those pills. But then I would think of that long list of side effects and the memory of our playful pantomiming would burst into my mind. By interrupting the flow of miserable thoughts my mind could refocus, and I usually found myself laughing all over again.

If I still felt like I needed some extra support, I would give Monte a call. With his ready boost of encouragement, my depression would dissipate enough that I would decide to wait on the pills. A few months later, I realized I was feeling much more hopeful and optimistic. Though I still experienced plenty of down times, when the prescription expired two years later, I threw the pills away without having taken a single one.

I hasten to add that I know this is not the right approach for everyone. Bodies and minds are all unique, and many people find relief from depression only after taking medication. However, in my particular situation, medication wasn't necessary.

I gained a better understanding of why that was when I read the book, *Feeling Good*, by Dr. David Burns. My friend who originally told me about the book said her doctor had helped her get off all three of her depression medications after 15 years of constant use. She learned to recognize her negative thinking and counter her destructive thoughts with more truthful, empowering ones.

Dr. Burns referred to studies which showed that in many cases, cognitive therapy, or changing thought patterns, is equally as effective and long lasting as taking medication. Since my depression had largely stemmed from my fearful thinking, when my negative thought patterns were interrupted, I was able to feel more hopeful and could handle things better.

Besides interrupting my negative patterns with humor, I discovered I could find a significant measure of relief from my depression by participating in sports. Since I had loved playing softball when I was younger, I joined the church's softball team for women shortly after we moved to our new home. Then we organized a coed softball team that included our husbands. Our games and practices provided me with a welcome distraction from the stress my perfectionism invited into my life.

Volleyball was introduced in our stake a few years later and our ward leaders encouraged us to form a team. We practiced on Tuesday and Thursday mornings and had games every Thursday evening. Though I had rarely played volleyball in my youth, I quickly fell in love with the sport and took advantage of every opportunity to play. For me, volleyball was like a drug with no side effects. An invigorating game helped me forget my worries and could give me a sunny outlook for many hours, and sometimes even several days.

Another thing that helped diffuse the depression was a change in my assignment at church. I was asked to be camp director for the young women. Being in the mountains nurtures my soul like few other things, and the prospect of helping young women experience that feeling filled me with wonderful anticipation. It was a demanding responsibility, but serving with Tracy, the president of the young women's organization, was a huge bonus. She was talented and funny, she adored the girls, and her delightful sense of humor spilled over into everything we did.

For a time, some of the clouds seemed to be drifting away from my path. I enjoyed our children's personalities and occasionally felt there just might be some hope for a joyful afterlife together in the Celestial Kingdom. Even though David said he hated going to church because a certain boy in his class constantly degraded him, my friends said that teenagers often go through an anti-church phase, and they assured me he would eventually grow out of it. After a while, I agreed to let him skip church because forcing him to go became too much of a battle for both of us.

During one intense discussion, David emphatically told me he didn't want to go on a mission. From the beginning of our marriage, Monte and I had planned on sending all of our sons on missions, but at that moment I was distinctly prompted to tell David I didn't want him to go on a mission unless he had a strong desire to go. I told him I'd seen the havoc created by unwilling missionaries who only went to please their parents and I had no interest in being a part of it. That wasn't actually what I wanted to say to him, but I knew I needed to say it, whether I liked it or not. I sensed God was trying to teach me about agency even though I really wasn't ready to listen.

# 15

# LIGHTNING STRIKES

*David announces he is gay*

Our lives seemed to be moving forward, albeit rather fitfully, until one beautiful spring day in 1988 when everything came to a screeching halt. It was a day that would change my life forever. David was now sixteen. From time to time I still caught little glimpses of his tender spirit, but his behavior during the previous few years had created enormous amounts of conflict in our family. He was an independent thinker who boldly expressed his opinions about everything, but on this day he seemed nervous and unsure as he approached me.

"Mom," he said quietly, "I want to tell you something before you hear it from someone else." Then he continued in a bolder voice as if he were reciting words he had practiced many times. "I'm gay. I've known it for a long time. All my friends are gay. I just want you to know before someone else tells you."

I stood in stunned silence, unable to catch my breath. Our eyes met and David paused for a moment as if he had more to say, but then he turned and ran out the front door. A car door slammed, an engine roared, and just like that, he was gone.

I slumped into a nearby chair feeling as if I had suddenly entered a twilight zone. At first, I couldn't wrap my mind around what he'd just told me, but as the implications of his words began to sink in, my thoughts went wild. "What are we going to do? We can't tell anyone! We have to move away and not let anyone know where we are going. We can't let our new neighbors know we are Latter-day Saints. I've failed God and I've failed my family."

At the time, I knew very little about homosexuality. I mostly knew I was afraid of it and I wanted to stay as far away from anything related to it as possible. A couple of years earlier, during an earnest conversation, David had caught me off guard when he'd asked what I thought of homosexuals. I remember telling him I was sure God loved them because He loves all His children, but that trouble always follows them, so he needed to avoid them. Now, here he was telling me that he was one of them.

I felt an urgency to pray, to seek some kind of guidance or comfort, but I couldn't find the words to begin. What could I possibly say to God? My greatest fear was now my reality. I had failed Him in my most important calling, because as everyone in the church has repeatedly heard, "No success in life can compensate for failure in the home." And even in the unlikely event that the rest of our family could someday make it to the Celestial Kingdom, there would always be that painful reminder of an "empty chair" at our celestial table.

Eventually, I collected myself enough to pick up the phone and call Monte, my faithful fix-it man. Sobbing, I tried to explain to him what had just happened and told him we needed to move away as soon as possible. He tried to calm me down and sort out what I was saying, but being rational was beyond me. Finally, he said he needed to get back to work and we would talk about everything when he got home.

As the fog began to lift from my mind, I searched for any possibility that might ease the trauma David's words had created. Finally, I concluded he must be mistaken. Surely, he just *thought* he was gay, but in reality, he really wasn't. If I could just talk to him and help him understand the error of his thinking, everything would be okay again. Until then, we must tell absolutely no one. I had worked so hard to protect our family image. People would be utterly shocked if they heard about this.

However, after several long and pleading conversations, David was still not convinced that he was wrong about his feelings. The counseling sessions we arranged for him didn't change his mind either. To find some hope, insight, and guidance for ourselves, Monte and I made an appointment with the same counselor.

The counselor informed us of studies which concluded that homosexuality was a result of fathers not bonding strongly enough with their sons during their early years. I sat there feeling sorry for Monte until the counselor went on to say that the problem was also the result of domineering mothers. Though more recent studies refute both of those conclusions, at the time, I viewed his words as more evidence that I was a total failure.

Monte's response to our counseling session was completely different from mine. When I asked him if he felt bad he simply said, "I can't change the past. I can only change the future." He prayerfully studied the scriptures, and he also prayed for a greater understanding of homosexuality, asking God what he could do as a parent in our current situation.

He began inviting David to have lunch with him once a week, and whenever David was home in the evening, he asked him if he'd like to play ping pong. Monte soon bought a pool table, hoping David would enjoy sharing that activity as well. While Monte was working to seek God's guidance and improve his relationship with David, I was sinking further and further into a dark abyss.

I had struggled with the darkness of depression before this crisis, but now my world went totally black. I cried endlessly, constantly asking myself what I had done wrong. How had I let our son's life turn into such a tragedy? Maybe if I hadn't been so cross, maybe if I hadn't been so busy with my church responsibilities, maybe if we hadn't let him get a job, maybe if I had listened more, maybe if I had been more understanding. The questions and self-accusations went on and on.

In the following days and weeks, I prayed endlessly, but I felt no connection to God. Though I now realize that He didn't abandon me during those difficult months, at the time I simply could not let go of my pain long enough to receive His comfort. Sometimes I would read from my scriptures, but I could find no answers. Every night my tears soaked my pillow.

The words to one of my favorite children's songs often flowed through my mind as I wept. "Heavenly Father, are you really there?" Occasionally I felt a fleeting moment of comfort as the second part of the song played through my mind. "Pray. He is there. Speak. He is listening. You are His child. His love now surrounds you." But when I got to the part, "He hears your prayers," I felt betrayed. He obviously was not hearing mine!

Keeping this new development a secret left me feeling isolated and lonely, but I was too ashamed of my failure to talk about it with anyone. Who could I tell? Our family image would be destroyed, and I was sure people would shun or even persecute David if they knew the truth. My life felt heavy and exhausting in every way—physically, mentally, spiritually, and especially emotionally.

It became apparent that Monte, my wonderful "fix-it" man, had no way of fixing this problem for me. He tenderly wrapped his arms around me as I cried myself to sleep each night, but this new development was definitely bigger than both of us. There was no hope that Monte would somehow be able to make it all better as he had so many times before.

Darkness prevailed as the tearful days dragged into months. I refused to write anything in my journal because putting it on paper made it seem more real and irreversible. Getting out of bed became almost impossible. If I felt like I absolutely had to go somewhere, I tried to deaden my mind, put on my happy face, and act as if everything was normal and wonderful.

I hated the feeling of living a lie again, but I knew of no other way to manage my pain. My intense wish to die returned, along with a myriad of suicidal thoughts. Of course, I felt guilty because I knew it wouldn't be right to abandon my husband and children, but in my distorted state of mind, I felt like everyone would be better off without me.

My thoughts were consumed by my failure as a mother and by my worries for our family. Having a gay son would undoubtedly make life miserable not just for David, but for everyone. The kids didn't like the way David treated them, but they loved him, and depended on the stability and wholeness of our family. How would they cope with the inevitable judgment and cruel comments? It seemed we were all destined to remain trapped in a world of endless misery.

In my heart, I knew God was our only hope, but my constant pleadings to Him brought no comfort. How could I persuade

Him to perform the miracle I thought we needed? More than anything in the world I wanted Him to "fix" David and make things right again.

Every evening when Monte got home from work, I would resume my painful chatter, as if another conversation would somehow bring a glimmer of hope to our situation. At first, Monte was patient and supportive, allowing me to go on and on about my overwhelming worries. However, after a while, he couldn't deal with it anymore. He began reminding me that nothing had changed since our last conversation and there was no point in rehashing the same thing over and over again.

Though I knew he was right, I didn't know what else I could do about it, and it felt like I had to be doing something. Monte encouraged me to seek counseling, but I couldn't see how that would help, considering our previous experience. Without Monte listening to me every day, the pain felt even more unbearable. I wondered how a person could hurt this much and not die.

While I lay in bed, the kids managed to get themselves fed and off to school each morning, popping into my room to kiss me goodbye or to get my signature on a permission slip. I felt incredibly guilty, but I could not muster the will to get up and face the day. Not until I realized my children were coming home from school in the same dirty clothes they had worn for the past three days, did I decide I simply *had* to get some kind of help.

The person I finally chose to talk to was our family doctor. He seemed to be the safest option because he didn't live in our neighborhood, he didn't know our friends, and he was legally bound to keep his patients' information confidential. I revealed my secret to him amid a torrent of tears, and he responded sympathetically while admitting that he didn't really know much at all about homosexuality. Then he proceeded to tell me stories of other parents whose children were doing drugs and living promiscuous lives, bringing unknown or unclaimed grandchildren into the world. When he finished, he asked me if I thought my pain was any greater than the pain these other parents had to endure.

He concluded by saying I should be grateful it was my son and not my husband we were talking about since he knew of other women who were struggling with that situation. Okay, so there were obviously others who were suffering with as much or more pain, but that did *not* make me feel any better, nor did it solve my problem. What I really needed to know was how I could possibly find my way out of this dark cloud that was destroying my life.

Though I received no immediate comfort from my doctor, just speaking the words to him seemed to have broken a barrier. After that appointment, I was able to gather the courage I needed to tell my sister. She was aware of our earlier struggles with David and she wept with me as I shared my crushing pain. She assured me of her continued love for both of us and she began calling regularly, allowing me to talk freely about my grief for as long as I wanted to.

It hadn't seemed terribly risky to tell my sister about David since she lived hundreds of miles away, but telling someone in my neighborhood required more courage—courage I didn't seem to have. But the need to share my pain with others persisted, and I eventually swore my walking partner to secrecy and shared my sorrow with her. Sometime later I confided in Tracy, my friend who served with me at church. They were both wonderfully supportive.

What a gift it was to feel a sincere and generous outpouring of love instead of the harsh judgment I had expected. My sense of isolation and loneliness diminished, and I started functioning significantly better. However, the menacing clouds still engulfed my path. My son's situation had not changed, and consequently, I continued to struggle with feelings of hopelessness and despair.

# 16

# THE DAWNING OF
# A BEAUTIFUL NEW DAY

*A change of heart*

One day I was on the phone with my walking partner discussing the situation of one of our friends. She was planning to donate a kidney to her fifteen-year-old son, and I had heard that the surgery was much harder on the donor than on the recipient. "I don't know if I could do it," I said. "Not only will her recovery be long and difficult, but her younger children won't understand why she can't get out of bed to take care of them. That would be so hard. She really is making a huge sacrifice."

My words surprised her. "Sure it would be hard," she said, "but I'd do it in a heartbeat for any of my children, and so would you."

Without thinking, I heard myself reply, "I would for anyone but David."

Instantly, I was frozen in time, stunned by my own words. They left an icy chill as they echoed again and again through the corridors of my mind, "I would for anyone but David. I would for anyone but David. I would for anyone but David." A barely coherent goodbye escaped my lips, as piercing new words came clearly into my mind—words that seemed to come directly from the scriptures. "In the last days the hearts of mothers will turn cold." (See Matthew 24:12, 14 and 2 Tim. 3:1–3.)

The phone dropped from my hand and I crumpled to my knees sobbing. In my anguish I cried aloud, "Heavenly Father, is that really who I have become? Please don't let me be a cold-hearted mother." My heart was crushed—broken in a way I had never known before—and I lay on the floor weeping bitterly.

The tears continued to flow as I reflected on the overwhelming conflicts David forced me to deal with every day. He slept in every morning long after school started. He was constantly using horrible language and making life miserable for our younger children. He ignored his chores, stayed out late, and generally disrupted family life in every way imaginable. Surely most people would agree that my pain and frustration were justified. But even so, hearing myself say that I would deliberately let him die even though it was within my power to save his life was beyond shocking. As I lay in a heap with a completely broken heart and a truly contrite spirit, I could think of nothing to do except beg God to rescue me from this horrible nightmare.

Suddenly, gentle words flowed into my mind. "You are not a cold-hearted mother. You are just hurt."

I felt so relieved I wanted to jump up and shout for joy, but those tender words were only the beginning. Other less comforting words quickly followed. "But think of how much more David is hurting. You have friends and loved ones who support you. He has no one. He has been rejected by his family, by his Church, by everything he has known his whole life."

As I considered the truth of those words, a feeling of deep sadness crept over me—only this time my sadness was for

David instead of for myself. My heart swelled with a profound sense of compassion as I began to understand the depths of *his* pain and *his* suffering. "But Heavenly Father!" I cried. "What can I do? I don't understand enough about homosexuality to be a good mother for him!"

Clearly and tenderly more words flowed ever so gently into my mind, "*You don't have to understand. You just have to love.*"

My sadness instantly turned to joy. "Well, I can do that!" I shouted. "I can love!" For the first time in what seemed like forever, my heart was filled with hope. I had loved many troubled kids over the years—nieces, nephews, neighborhood kids, youth I had worked with in the church—I had loved them all. And infused with this new, vibrant, divine perspective, I suddenly felt confident in my ability to love my gay son.

As I lingered on my knees rejoicing, I immediately found myself immersed in a glorious sea of pure love. I felt it extending all around me, above and below and especially through me. Then I was struck by the sure knowledge that this same sweet, unconditional love extended not only to me, but to David, to all of his friends, and indeed, to every single one of God's children. Never had I experienced this kind of oneness with heaven and earth.

Every trace of fear, pain, and perfectionism vanished from my heart, replaced with an overflowing abundance of God's indescribable love. I didn't move. I didn't even want to breathe. I was experiencing a beautiful kind of love I hadn't even known existed. Oh how I wished I could make that moment last forever!

I stayed there for a very long time, and when I did eventually rise from the floor, I was no longer the same person. God's amazing love rose with me. Moment by moment, He showed me how to share His love with David. Where I previously would have felt depressed, impatient, or hurt about something, I now felt compassion and tenderness.

At first David was suspicious of his "new mother." He didn't trust my flood of affection, and wondered how long it would be before I returned to my old, critical ways. Opportunities for conflict continued to arise, but I was undeterred. This gift was too sweet to let slip away. I constantly prayed for guidance and the ability to retain the feelings of love that had so freely been given to me.

I fixed David's favorite foods and left notes if he didn't come home before I went to bed. I encouraged him to bring his friends home and I embraced them all, whether they had purple hair, gold nose rings, spiked leather jackets, chains draped across their shoulders, black lipstick, or all of those things combined. Each day as I drove David to school we engaged in pleasant conversation, even when he was late. Although I was tempted to chide him for his falling grades, when he explained how unsafe he felt at school, I realized it was actually not a good place for him to be. Eventually I helped him withdraw from his classes and we enrolled him in an alternate school. Before the end of the year he completed the requirements for his high school diploma.

Monte was thrilled with my change of heart, and our other children also enjoyed its benefits. As I lived my life through new eyes, I found greater and greater delight in the developing character and personality of each child. Trivial matters became much less likely to upset me, although I did occasionally revert back to my old perfectionistic habit of trying to control or fix things. But as soon as I realized what I was doing, I quickly checked myself. I was absolutely determined to maintain this amazing new-found freedom.

Even though we continued to encounter many challenges in dealing with David's attitudes and decisions, my life felt wonderfully peaceful. I had no idea where this new path was taking us, but I was optimistic. Regardless of where it might lead, I knew we would be okay because God was walking it with us.

A few months later I was sitting alone at my kitchen table reflecting contentedly on the recent changes in our lives when, from out of nowhere, an ominous voice jumped into my head. Its words were dark, foreboding, and persuasive. "But Elona, you can never be *truly* happy, because all of your children will never be married in the temple."

Suddenly I was back in that pit of blackness, drowning in a pool of despair. The words repeated relentlessly in my mind, "I'm never going to be happy. I'm never going to be happy. I'm *never* going to be happy." A feeling of complete hopelessness engulfed me, and in that moment, all my progress seemed to be swept away. Misery pressed heavily upon me, and I felt like I was suffocating, as if all the air had been sucked out of the room. Had all my recent peace and joy been a lie?

Suddenly something deep inside me snapped. I sprang from my chair and I heard my own voice shouting. "Oh yeah! I can't live if I can't be happy! I'm just going to have to be happy no matter what!"

This outburst struck me like a bolt of lightning. Every cell of my body felt vibrantly alive and tingly. I instantly knew beyond any doubt that my happiness was in my own hands. It didn't depend on my children, it didn't depend on my husband, and it didn't depend on my external circumstances. It didn't depend on anyone or anything else but me. It was a choice I alone had to make, and I chose to be happy.

This sure knowledge burned to the very core of my being. I had heard the concept before, but now I understood it in the very depths of my soul. I knew without question that I could be happy—not necessarily glad, but trusting, peaceful, hopeful, optimistic, okay—even when my children weren't doing what I wanted them to do. And furthermore, I could be happy even when my husband couldn't fix all the problems that came into my life.

Ultimately I realized that God was teaching me about the gift of choice. Although I don't get to choose what other people think or do, and I don't always get to choose the circumstances surrounding my life, I *can* choose how I think about them. I can choose how I let them influence my peace and happiness. Each of us has to make our own choices over and over again every day of our lives. I finally recognized and wholeheartedly accepted the gift and responsibility to choose, and I chose to be happy!

This experience blessed me with profound peace. It strengthened and comforted me when David, who was still only seventeen, insisted that he needed to move into his own apartment. Though my husband and I were both very concerned for him, we felt we should support his decision rather than demand that he stay in our home until he turned eighteen. We were thankful that he was leaving because *he* wanted to go, rather than because we were "throwing him out," which is what several people had encouraged us to do.

Still, it was hard to watch Monte help David load his bed, dresser, and other belongings into our van and then deposit them in a dark and barren apartment forty miles away from our home. David had a questionable roommate, no job, and far more freedom than I would have chosen for him. He seemed nervous and unsettled, but he was determined that this was what he wanted to do. Our farewell included a long embrace, repeated assurances of our love, and my pleading invitation for him to return home often.

Because David didn't have a car, he depended on his friends for transportation. Their visits were usually brief and somewhat strained, but I always tried to communicate my love each time they came. Hugs, food, and supplies for his apartment were among the few things I could offer. Sometimes the hugs felt a little awkward, especially for his friends, but I felt God's love for them and I wanted them to feel it too.

Each time David left and I felt the inevitable tugging at my heartstrings, I turned my thoughts back to the experiences that had brought me earlier peace. Armed with those memories, I could mentally and emotionally place David back in God's loving hands where I knew he belonged. It was not always easy, but it always worked.

After surviving on his own for a couple of difficult years, David packed all his worldly possessions into the little blue Mazda we had helped him purchase, and he drove twenty-five hours nonstop to Dallas. He stayed with a friend he had met a few months earlier, and within a week he found a job. He called every few weeks to share what was going on in his new life, and most of the time he seemed pretty happy. I wasn't at all surprised when he told me he and his friend had decided to become "partners."

Two years later, David and his partner moved to New York City. After the move, David didn't call as often, and when he did call, it was usually to talk about the details of his most recent struggles. Sometimes it was his work, sometimes his finances, sometimes his relationship, sometimes it was all three. Whenever he and his partner had major conflicts, he always called me for advice.

For the first few years following my "change of heart" experience, I felt the wonderful influence of God's unconditional love flowing through me every time I talked to David. The sun had burst through the clouds, and I joyfully received the warmth and clarity it brought. However, at some point, I began to notice that those pure feelings no longer came to me as automatically as they had before. In the midst of a difficult conversation, I would find myself pausing to choose words that would *seem* loving and supportive even though I didn't totally feel them.

Most challenging were the couple of times David came home to visit. He was always edgy and easily upset. When I finally admitted to myself that I was glad he lived far away so I didn't have to confront our differences all the time, I felt a deep sense of sadness and loss. Although it wasn't as obvious in my other relationships, that wondrous gift of constant, unconditional love had somehow slipped from my grasp.

# 17

# AN ANCHOR FOR ALL STORMS

*Developing my relationship with God*

As the years passed, I continued to rejoice in my change of heart experience and the awesome transformation it had made in my life. However, I missed the pure sweetness of God's amazing, unconditional love. Though I suspected that the scriptures held the key to regaining the divine connection I had so cherished, I just couldn't make myself study them consistently, no matter how hard I tried.

Then in February of 2001, I got a phone call from my sister. "I've found this wonderful book," she exclaimed, "and I know you are going to love it! It has totally changed my life!" She raved on, explaining that it was a Twelve-Step scripture study program written by a woman named Colleen Harrison and that it only required fifteen minutes of study time a day. She said as she had followed the program, her heart and mind had been joyously opened to God's love and guidance.

Not only did I find her enthusiasm irresistible, I was also instantly drawn to the book's title, *He Did Deliver Me from Bondage*. I had known bondage more than once in my life, and I had tasted the blessed sweetness of deliverance before. Now I was ravenously hungry to experience that sweetness again.

That evening I bought the book and began reading its introductory pages. The author's words were candid and direct. I immediately identified with her story of perfectionism and her misguided desires to *appear* to be the model Latter-day Saint woman.

Looking further, I found that I loved the format. Each chapter contained a discussion of one of the twelve steps and was followed by seven scripture passages, one for each day of the week. A related question accompanied each passage, and a blank space was provided for the answer. My written answers would become a daily journal of my personal thoughts and feelings. The appendix included a detailed discussion on the concept of pondering and seeking to understand how to apply the scriptures to personal situations in life.

The next morning I woke up early, filled with excitement, but then I suddenly started to worry that this might not work for me the way it had for my sister. Maybe I was expecting too much. Maybe I would end up disappointed. It would be awkward to tell my sister I had failed to duplicate her experience. Maybe I should wait and try it sometime later when I felt more confident.

But I didn't *want* to wait any longer, so gathering my determination I pushed the fears aside and knelt down to pray. I asked the Lord to help me receive the blessings the program had to offer me, and then I read through the introductory discussion and wrote down my thoughts about the first scripture as directed. I liked the idea of really pondering and searching my heart for the answer to a single question, and I liked knowing that I was only committed to giving it fifteen minutes a day even though I had spent a whole hour on it this first day.

By the end of the week, I had written seven thoughtful entries, and I felt a definite sense of accomplishment. The next day I read chapter two, which discussed Christ's redeeming power. Throughout the week I wrote out my thoughts and feelings about the tender, intimate messages contained in the assigned verses. As I wrote, a familiar Spirit quietly crept into my heart and filled me with the same amazing love that had healed my broken heart and lifted me from my pain and despair years earlier.

From those verses sprang an endless fountain of pure love that flowed gently into my soul. At last, I had found what I had been searching for all those years: a way to consistently reconnect with God's unconditional love. Scripture study suddenly became a joy rather than a chore. Day after day that feeling of incredible love drew me back to the process of praying, reading, pondering, and writing.

Each night I set my alarm so I would have extra time to study in the morning, but that proved to be unnecessary. I found myself bouncing out of bed long before the alarm sounded, anxious to take advantage of every available moment. I had to force myself to interrupt my study long enough to fix Monte's lunch and get him off to work. Then I would return to my books and continue to bask in the Spirit. Sometimes I spent hours at my desk capturing several verses or even a whole chapter in a single day.

I was like a thirsty garden that simply could not soak in enough water from that cool, refreshing spring. I drank deeply, even anxiously, fearing that this too might pass and I would be left thirsting again. But the fountain flowed endlessly, merrily, without any sense of urgency—there for the taking each time I returned. As I read, I asked God to help me understand His words and show me how He would like me to apply them in my life. Soon I was calling the scriptures my "love notes from God" because I found them so full of loving messages.

At first I said my morning prayer facing the picture window in our living room because I loved watching the first rays of dawn break over the mountains. But before long I retreated to my office. The office window still faced the morning light, but there I could shut the door and feel confident that I was completely alone with God. There I could pray out loud without distractions, and I could also assume whatever prayer posture suited me at the moment. Most often I was on my knees, but sometimes I would be lying on my back. Many times I would kneel and reach my arms up to God or out to my sides as I imagined myself trying to catch all the blessings he was pouring down upon me.

The privacy helped me focus on what I was feeling, and on the things my heart desired to communicate to God. Sometimes I would pick up my scriptures and just stroke the columns of words, or lift them to my cheek and rest my face on the open pages. Anyone watching might have thought I was a little crazy, but I felt joyful! I couldn't get enough of God's love. I was on a quest to nourish my starving soul.

Sometimes I felt an outpouring of love that literally took my breath away. Other times I was given thoughts that taught me how to love my husband and children better. Sometimes a friend or relative came to mind and I was prompted to reach out to them in a particular way. Sometimes I was given a sense of calmness about a difficult situation involving other friends and loved ones. Whatever the challenge, I turned to God for peace and guidance. If an answer didn't come right away, I didn't worry because I felt secure in God's love and confident that He would be with me.

Throughout our marriage, Monte and I had knelt on opposite sides of our bed at night and silently said our personal prayers at the same time. I always felt like I needed to finish my prayer when he finished his so we could talk before going to bed. Now I felt the need to be alone for this personal prayer too, so I again retreated to the office. I didn't want to just say a prayer, I wanted to truly connect with God and sincerely thank Him for my life and the bounteous blessings of each day. I appreciated Monte'x patience with my longer prayers, and he appreciated the changes taking place in me.

The office doubled as our guest room, so whenever we had company I gathered my books and retreated to the storage room so I still had the privacy I needed for my prayers at night and my study in the morning. If for some reason I missed the early morning study time, I looked for an opportunity to study later in the day, even if it was only a few minutes before going to bed at night. God was opening my heart and renewing my soul as never before. I had a whole reservoir of love to draw on whenever I ran into difficult situations. It was a beautiful approach to everything that came into my life.

My earlier stress over scripture study melted away. I realized it didn't matter that I couldn't remember references or piece together every point of doctrine. It was no longer about the intellectual aspects of scripture study for me. Now it was all about connecting with God and feeling His love and guidance.

As I returned to the scriptures each day, I was filled with a sense of wonder at God's acceptance of me exactly as I was, even without fixing any of my faults and flaws. I knew He cherished me totally and completely, and no other opinion of me was important. I didn't have to keep trying to be good enough. Of course, I knew He wanted me to continue to grow and improve in my ability to love, but I didn't have to *do* more or *be* more to be worthy of His love. I discovered that *I am already enough because I am His child.* I constantly rejoiced in His love as I continued writing the thoughts and feelings that flooded my heart and mind.

Wonderful, calming peace permeated my life as I released my need for the approval of others and embraced God's love and acceptance of me. For a short time I felt concerned because it almost seemed like I was distancing myself from other people, including Monte, but gradually the eyes of my understanding were opened to the truth. I was actually just shifting my faith to God, where it had always belonged, and releasing my expectations of others.

I found I no longer needed Monte to be my fix-everything man. I no longer needed my children to be different than they were. I no longer needed my sisters or friends to tell me I was worthwhile. My prayers were no longer that God would fix me or anyone else, but that I would be able to freely receive His love, and freely share it with everyone around me.

I found I could love Monte—and everyone else—more completely when my love for God anchored my life. My love for others did not depend on their behavior or their ability to serve me. I just felt love for them. Of course, I recognized that it wasn't *my* love that created the miracle. It was God's love flowing through me. Each night I went to bed joyfully filled with gratitude and wonder for God's mercy and grace that day. What a glorious relief from the ruthless criticizing, analyzing, and evaluating that had ruled my bedtime for so many years!

As I approached the end of the study guide, I feared that I wouldn't be able to maintain this delicious and nourishing connection with God on my own. What would I do when I didn't have the author's questions to prompt my contemplations? How would I know what to write in my spiritual journal? How could I keep this wonderful feeling without having someone tell me what to do every step of the way?

After finishing the last lesson, I tentatively ventured out on my own. I immediately realized I didn't have anything to worry about. Whether I focused on a few verses or a whole chapter, by following the pattern of praying, reflecting on the words I read, asking questions, and writing the thoughts that came to me, I continued to feel an outpouring of God's love and guidance.

Most days passed quite uneventfully, but I treasured feeling connected with God, and the joy of just being alive. I was constantly thanking God for little things like the smile of a child at the grocery store, or my husband's kiss as he came through the door after work, or a stimulating conversation with a friend. When things happened that threw me back into my old perfectionistic thought patterns, I always turned to God and asked Him to help me regain my perspective and center myself in His love.

For example, one Sunday evening a neighbor knocked on my door and said he had a concern about my interaction with him and a couple of other people at church that day. He told me he had previously heard others say that my "over-exuberance" bothered them, but up until this experience, he had never had a problem with it. However, he felt I needed to know that he thought my enthusiasm that day had been inappropriate.

I was dumbfounded! Here was a man I held in the highest regard telling me that some unmentioned number of people were bothered by my enthusiasm. Furthermore, as a result of my behavior that day, he had joined their ranks.

He continued by saying he had come over to talk to me about it rather than secretly harboring bad feelings. His words made me nervous and an awkward silence followed, but I invited him into the living room.

As we began to discuss our differing perspectives of the situation, we each realized there had been some misunderstandings on both of our parts. The awkwardness melted away, and by the time he left, our friendship didn't seem to be any worse for the wear. Unfortunately, my thoughts insisted on returning to his initial comments, and that's when the trouble began.

Who were these unnamed people who had bad feelings toward me? Were my offenses recent or did they date back to my service with him in the scout troop years ago? I was unquestionably enthusiastic about scouting! Did a huge number of church members think I was too exuberant or were there just a few? Even though I kept trying not to go there, all evening I felt myself falling into the old perfectionism trap of wanting everyone to have a favorable opinion of me.

When I woke up the next morning, I felt less agitated, but for some reason, my mind was not yet ready to let go. I tried praying and reading my scriptures, but peace continued to elude me. Finally, I decided to try journaling. I began to write out all the details of the incident, hoping for some wonderful, calming insight.

After several minutes of trying to pinpoint exactly what was going on in my head, a wave of impatience swept over me and my focus changed. I began to write about how sick I was of trying to figure out my feelings, and about how foolish it was to spend so much time and energy on something that didn't matter. My thoughts began to shift, directing me toward God's love and His desire to bless me with joy and peace. I wrote about how much goodness there is in my life and about how I didn't have to let this experience—or others like it—affect me.

As I reflected on my love for God and my trust in Him, the tension in my soul gently dissolved. I no longer felt concerned or irritated about the incident. The Spirit reminded me that everyone has their own opinions, but their opinions are not my business. It was over. Case closed. Thank you, God!

It was lovely to be thinking clearly again, to be living freely, loving joyfully, and rejoicing in the Lord. I realized it had only been about twelve hours since my neighbor had come to my door, and during most of those hours, I had been asleep! What a wonderful contrast to the time when a similar incident would have kept me in knots for months, or even years.

Day after day I was amazed by the multitude of little miracles I noticed in my life. I was equally amazed that I never tired of my morning scripture study. When I lost my routine because of a trip or some other interruption, instead of losing my enthusiasm, I found I couldn't wait to get back to my regular schedule. It anchored my life and prepared me for the next approaching storm.

# 18

# TESTING THE ANCHOR

*David moves back home*

Several weeks before the attack on the World Trade Center in September of 2001, I got a phone call from David. He still lived in New York, but things were not going well. He was struggling with his business, his relationship, and his health. We discussed the possibility of him coming home for a bit so he could get well before beginning a different job, but there were new factors to consider. "It wouldn't be easy for you," I warned. "You know Grandma is living with us now, and you also know how she feels about homosexuality."

He wasn't anxious to step into that hornet's nest so we left the conversation hanging, but after the Trade Center tragedy, David's business collapsed completely. His partner, who was out of town visiting family at the time, called and said he no longer wanted to live in New York, and he no longer wanted to be in the relationship. Alone and in financial distress, David called to pursue our earlier conversation.

"I have a couple of relocation possibilities that look pretty good," he told me. "I just need to come home and work on my health for a few weeks while I figure out whether to go to Colorado or to California. Grandma and I can survive that long. I can sleep on the floor in the family room and just stay out of her way."

Monte and I both wondered what "a few weeks" might actually turn out to be. We had heard plenty of horror stories about adult children returning home. It was certainly contrary to what we had always imagined for our children. We had assisted each of them with college expenses so they could live in an apartment and experience life on their own before starting their careers and their own families. Our hope had been to help them become independent, happy adults who would never need to live under our roof again. But in the end, after much discussion and prayer, we both felt we should welcome David back into our home.

Coming home proved to be an extremely difficult adjustment for David. It brought up a lot of anger about his past and about the way Monte and I had raised him. As his health issues persisted and his job possibilities faded, the hostility between him and my mother escalated. Everyone in the house walked on eggshells. At any moment something could—and often did—explode between them.

David seemed driven to confront me about every difficulty he had faced in his childhood, and we spent countless hours engaged in intense conversation. Sometimes he angrily demanded that I justify the way I had parented him in specific situations, but I found I could calmly flow with his barrage of emotions as I maintained my pattern of consistent prayer, scripture study, and journaling. I could listen to his accusations without feeling attacked and was often guided to offer an apology and ask for his forgiveness. Monte was amazed at my ability to maintain a sense of inner peace through it all, and I was actually quite amazed myself. But I clearly recognized that it was a divine gift and not something I could ever have conjured up on my own.

While living in New York, David had embraced Tibetan Buddhism and in our calmer moments we discovered that we had many beliefs in common. He shared a set of tapes with me about the principles of Buddhism and we had some great conversations about them. But we still had very different perspectives on most political and religious issues, which seemed to cause endless turmoil for him.

For a long time after he came home, David tried to be careful not to use offensive language, even during our most tempestuous conversations. However, on one occasion I made a comment about an event from his teenage years which triggered not only fierce emotion but also a long string of foul language. Obviously, some intense pain still surrounded the memory that replayed in his mind.

In earlier years I had felt responsible for every word that came out of my children's mouths, and I had imposed severe consequences for swearing, crude language, and name-calling. But now I listened as my son raged for several minutes, doing my best to hear him with my heart, silently asking God to help me communicate His pure love to David. Finally, I extended my hand and touched his shoulder. He resisted for a few seconds but then moved closer, allowing me to wrap my arms around him.

As I held him close, his breathing slowed and his body relaxed into my embrace. "I'm truly sorry you felt so abandoned and vulnerable when that happened," I said quietly. "It must have been terrifying." His demeanor softened, and we began to talk about the pain that still festered inside him from those unhealed wounds. It never occurred to me to reprimand him for the words he had used to express his pain.

Not long after that, David and I were in the middle of another impassioned discussion when he suddenly stopped and pensively studied my face. After a very long pause, he finally spoke. "Mom," he said, "you practice your religion differently now."

"You're right," I replied softly. "It's because I understand my religion differently now."

I've had countless opportunities to practice my religion differently since I experienced the healing power of God's pure love all those years ago. My religion has become a religion of love and joy instead of fear and judgment. I know I can connect with God's love and trust Him to bless me for my efforts instead of cursing me for being imperfect. I know that even with my perfectionistic tendencies, I can live from a place of love and come back to that love when I get off track. I'm so grateful I know that there can be peace for perfectionists through God's love.

While David was in New York he started smoking, and he brought that habit home with him. In earlier years I would have been distraught and felt compelled to frequently remind him about the useless expense of tobacco and the harm it causes the human body. But I no longer felt any inclination to lecture him, even though my beliefs and values had not changed. David did try to be especially considerate of me when he smoked. Not only did he go outside, but he also tried to make sure I didn't see him smoking.

One night when he came into the kitchen I could tell he was feeling particularly troubled. My heart ached for him as I watched him walk out the back door, and I wondered if there might be something I could do to ease his pain. I quickly finished what I was doing and followed him out onto the deck. He noticed me approaching just as he lit his cigarette. "Mom," he said through the darkness, "don't come out. I'm smoking, and I know you don't like to see me smoke."

"I know, Honey," I said quietly. "And I appreciate your thoughtfulness. But it's okay."

Sitting down next to him on the swing, I leaned my head into his shoulder and rested my hand on his knee. We rocked back and forth in silence until he finished the cigarette. Then he slowly began to pour out his grief. The smell of tobacco lingered on the still night air, but it didn't claim my attention. My only focus was his sorrow. I felt honored that he would allow me to sit beside him in that moment and share the pain he was feeling.

Even after months and months of hashing through all of David's anger about childhood experiences and how he was raised, turmoil continued to fill his life. Gay issues came up frequently in the news or with his friends, and whenever they did, there would be another explosion—or many explosions. He didn't know how to manage his anger, and I didn't know how to help him. He spent a lot of time talking on the phone with his friends about all the injustices gays were experiencing and who was to blame for them. Although I tried to communicate my love and support for him and for those who were suffering, to a large degree I seemed to represent the enemy. He and his friends considered my church and my church leaders to be the source of most of their problems.

Over and over he vented his frustration and anger to me about gay suicides, about Proposition 8 in California, about businesses refusing to serve gay couples, about how the courts were handling gay issues, and about things said in churches around the country. He became less restrained in the words he chose to express his feelings, and many times I found myself listening to an onslaught of foul and venomous language. To weather these storms, I tenaciously clung to the anchor of God's love for me and for David. A few times Monte and I seriously considered telling him he had to move out, but each time I prayed about it, I felt certain we needed to wait.

In spite of all the turmoil, David clearly had a lot to offer others. Some of his lengthy phone conversations were devoted to helping people work through their personal challenges. While he invariably dominated the conversation when he and I were talking, he would patiently listen to the details of a problem someone else was experiencing. Drawing from his own experiences and his vast study of energy work while he was New York, he could almost always shed new light on a particular challenge, helping both friends and new acquaintances work through troubling emotions and situations. At least two of his friends credit him with saving their lives, and numerous others have told me his insights have blessed and lifted their lives immeasurably.

Despite the many difficulties we went through, much healing has taken place since David came home. The years have given him the opportunity to develop his relationships with his siblings and their children. Of course, relationships are always in flux, and family gatherings can be a bit complicated for him, but sometimes he chooses to join us for special celebrations and activities. He enjoys cooking and will occasionally share an international recipe with the family. He makes up delightful stories for our grandchildren, and he offers valuable insights which expand my understanding and perspective.

One of my favorite miracles was the eventual transformation of David's relationship with my mother. Although I expected some friction between them when he returned home, having the two of them under the same roof created far more conflict than I had ever imagined. From the beginning, the tension was palpable every time they were in the same room. As far as I could tell, they didn't even attempt to be civil to each other.

My diligent efforts to smooth things over did little to resolve their conflicts. For years I went back and forth between them trying to help them see each other in a kinder light. One day after failing to mitigate yet another heated exchange between them, I finally surrendered. Throwing my hands in the air I exclaimed, "Go ahead and kill each other if you must! I obviously can't make you be nice to one another!" After that, I did my best to stay out of their conflicts even though they both continued to bring their complaints to me.

They went through some pretty rough times, but gradually they managed to work things out. At first, it was only mutual tolerance, but later they became less defensive and were often quite pleasant with each other. As Mother lost some of her physical strength, she also seemed to lose some of her edginess. Meanwhile, David gradually developed a feeling of respect for Mother and an appreciation for her skills and talents. He softened even further as he watched her face the increasing challenges of old age.

Somewhere along the way, I was surprised to notice an element of tenderness growing between them. Mother started inviting David to share treats people brought for her, and she also expressed her appreciation when he did little things to help her. David began clearing her dishes after dinner and would occasionally bring her thoughtful little gifts. Every now and then he could be seen outside in the yard helping her with a project, and sometimes she could be found in the kitchen coaching him through a culinary skill he was trying to master.

As Mother's health continued to decline, David became more and more attentive to her. She finally began to understand his sense of humor, and would laugh in pure delight when he teased her. I often heard her thank him when he took a meal to her room or helped her find a show she wanted to watch on her television. He sometimes went by her door just to say hello and would offer to help if she needed something.

To my amazement, David became one of Mother's most trusted caregivers. His willingness to attend to her needs was a huge blessing in my life. When I had to leave her for an appointment or some other commitment, he made sure she was well taken care of. Without his help, I would have often been left searching for someone to stay with her in my absence.

The sweet bond which eased its way into their hearts reminded me that with God, nothing is impossible. It also gave me a new appreciation for both of them, and for their individual journeys. Even back in my days of unchecked perfectionism, I never would have dared imagine such a miracle. There was just too much to fix. But sometimes God has his own sneaky way of making miracles, and eventually, those dark clouds could no longer restrain the glorious sunshine of His love. Our lives were all greatly enriched by the gentle warmth of this unexpected miracle which had risen from seemingly insurmountable differences.

19

# FURTHER TESTING
# OF THE ANCHOR

*More unexpected challenges*

If I were creating a movie of my journey, I would probably choose to end it right here. Most people like movies that wrap up nicely, and since the long-standing conflict between David and Mother had been resolved, we were enjoying a sweet season of peace in our home.

But unlike movies, life goes on. Sometimes we have a pretty good idea of what might be waiting for us around the next bend in the road. Other times we suddenly find ourselves in the middle of a stormy surprise. To navigate those difficult times and continue to live joyfully, we need to discover and develop some anchoring tools we can quickly turn to. We sometimes discover them in books or by watching other people, but our most powerful tools seem to develop from our own experience.

In telling my story, I've shared how I discovered tools that have been very beneficial to me. The most significant one would undoubtedly be immersing the world in God's love. Others include managing my thoughts, embracing reality, cultivating gratitude, and maintaining a relationship of trust with God. I affectionately call these tools "my stepping stones to joy" because I rely heavily on them to lift my spirit and help me stay in—or return to—a place of peace and joy. (You can see a list of my stepping stones at the end of this book. A more lengthy explanation and examples can be found in my upcoming book, *Stepping Stones to Joy: 12 Tools for Managing Perfectionism and Living Joyfully.*)

After my mother passed away in the fall of 2016, things unfolded much as I expected. It required minimal effort to take care of her affairs since she had no possessions of any real monetary value and only a few sentimental treasures to distribute among family members. Of course, her passing did change the routine of my life dramatically. I missed her deeply, and for months I found myself riding an emotional roller coaster.

Once Mother's affairs were settled, I expected to be devoting the majority of my time to grandchildren, my writing, and other projects I'd been procrastinating. But David's situation quickly became my foremost concern. After all these years, he was still living in our basement and I felt it was way past time for him to get a job and move out. In fact, we'd had numerous conversations about that long before Mother had left us.

David was clearly intelligent enough to earn a living, and he had plenty of other talents and abilities, but no career path had materialized over the years even though Monte and I had encouraged and supported him in a variety of business attempts and other interests. He often talked about things he wanted to do when he had his own home, so I couldn't understand why he didn't take the bull by the horns, get a job, and find his own place to live.

During the last couple of years I had paid for a number of online business classes and courses for him, and we set up weekly meetings to discuss what he was learning and how it was helping him progress toward employment. When we met, he talked in lengthy generalities, but rarely got to anything specific. I tried to help him focus on incremental steps he could take, but no matter how carefully I chose my words, our discussions almost always ended in conflict. He felt like I didn't recognize or appreciate his efforts and I felt like we were spinning our wheels in the same old rut.

Menacing clouds threatened to destroy my peace, and at times they undoubtedly obscured my vision. However, by calling heavily on my stepping stones to joy, I was able to hang onto hope and live in a place of peace in spite of the clouds. For months I puzzled and pondered. I knew something needed to change, but I didn't know exactly what it was or how it needed to happen.

My suggestions continued to be met with resistance and defensiveness, but I was encouraged when David accepted the opportunity to do on-call work for a developing company. Although he only earned a few hundred dollars a month, it gave him a chance to address some of his concerns about getting back into the workforce. While he found some aspects of the job quite stressful, he liked his boss and co-workers and he enjoyed getting out of the house. He was glad to have a fairly consistent income to pay for his phone and the minimal rent we were charging him.

Through the years I had occasionally encouraged David to check into a twelve-week course at the local university which had helped one of my friends get back into the workforce. I didn't really know anything about the course except that when my friend took it, she got the support she needed to deal with her fear of failure and she went back to school. When she finished her degree a few years later, her confidence had grown immensely and we joyously celebrated her graduation. She soon found a job she enjoyed and has been working in her chosen field ever since.

Because of my friend's experience, I thought the course might help David find a good career path, but whenever I mentioned it, he never expressed any interest. However, timing can make all the difference. One day, when David came home from his on-call job feeling distraught, exhausted, and discouraged, the course my friend had taken popped into my mind again. Grabbing my purse, I slapped a $20 bill on the table. I told David the money was his as soon as he made one little phone call to find out if the class was still available and when it might be starting again.

The next morning he was on the phone talking to a pleasant and helpful receptionist who told him another course was beginning the following week. She said he would be welcome to join it . . . as long as he could fit in a two-hour screening interview the next day to verify that he met the required enrollment criteria.

David was nervous about stepping into an unfamiliar situation that would require him to be up early twice a week, but he was willing to go and check it out. During his interview, the woman told him he not only qualified for the class, but that she was certain he would find it very beneficial. She also suggested he call and make an appointment with Vocational Rehab, a support program run by the state of Utah.

The next Tuesday I dropped David off for his first class. When I picked him up three hours later I could tell this was going to be an adventure. He was anxious and agitated about assignments he had to do before his class on Thursday, but he enjoyed the teacher and was clearly interested in supporting the other students. A few days later he contacted Vocational Rehab, was assigned a caseworker, and made an appointment to see her.

When David met with his caseworker, she explained several wonderful services the program offered. However, she said he would have to apply for assistance at Workforce Services, another state program, to be eligible for most of them. She also said he needed to have an initial evaluation with a therapist and she scheduled the appointment for him that very day.

With so many wheels suddenly in motion, David felt overwhelmed and overstimulated. I, on the other hand, felt excited and grateful. Finally, he was getting the support I had not been able to give him. After each class or therapy session, he always needed a patient, listening ear and lots of encouragement. Sometimes it took days for him to unwind and talk through everything that had been triggered, but I was happy to be there for him because this was obviously a step in the right direction.

The therapist's evaluation was slow in coming, but eventually David received an email with the results. It said he had severe anxiety, depression, and some learning disabilities, along with symptoms of other unspecified disorders. The therapist recommended seeing a physician for medical advice and engaging in a program of psychotherapy to assist with symptoms of anxiety and depression.

Just before David's class ended, one of his friends in New York asked him to come out for a couple of weeks and work on his apartment with him. David was excited for the break, but I felt concerned that he would lose his momentum. Going to New

York meant he would have to postpone the next class which he had already signed up for, and it would disrupt the flow of his rehab appointments and therapy sessions. It also meant he would miss several work opportunities. As he prepared for his trip, I called on my stepping stones many times to help me stay in a place of peace.

David enjoyed being in New York again. In fact, he enjoyed it so much that he extended his trip from two weeks to six, and then from six to ten, each time postponing his classes and therapy even more. Over and over my thoughts invited me to worry about whether he would be willing to jump back into his program when he returned, but I kept reminding myself to trust God and to use my stepping stones. There was no point in stressing about things I had no control over.

During this time God offered me some inspiration about how I could assist David in moving forward. I felt prompted to pursue our previous idea of setting up a little kitchenette in the basement for David. Since we had already bought a couple of used cabinets, I called a plumber, purchased a few feet of countertop, and figured out how we could fit a little fridge and other small appliances into the tiny space. It turned out to be a fun project, and I was especially excited when we were able to get the sink and fridge installed the day before David returned.

Another unexpected bit of guidance was to move forward with the purchase of a new car so David could use my old one. Monte and I had been talking about getting a new car for over a year and had even done some test driving several months earlier, but I loved my old car and was in no hurry to break in a new one. Meanwhile, David had been taking the bus to work, to class, and to therapy appointments, which seemed appropriate since he couldn't afford to buy his own car. I always picked him up when he worked an evening shift because the bus didn't run that late, and I drove him to class or to his appointments if his schedule was too tight to take the bus. It wasn't always convenient for me to take him, but I was glad he was making an effort to progress and I was eager to support him. Now God seemed to want him to have even more freedom to take care of himself. So we bought the new car.

David came home tired and a bit edgy. He wasn't immediately comfortable with the idea of having a car available to him because he said it felt like too much responsibility. He said he was still processing his trip, and talked to me at length about people he had met, places he had visited, and the work he had done on his friend's apartment. He also spent a lot of time in his room sleeping, talking on the phone, and meditating.

Although he liked the little kitchenette, he was nervous about how much his food was going to cost and about using the small appliances. He said he knew this would be good practice for him before moving out, but after a week, he still hadn't cooked anything down there. When we had our weekly meeting the following Tuesday, I gave him a list of simple meal possibilities and challenged him to try one little thing each day. I hoped the list would help get him started, but just reading through it overwhelmed him, and we were immediately enmeshed in another conflict.

I had assumed David would want to be the first to cook in his new little kitchen, but a few days later when I offered to show him how to make noodles in his rice cooker, he gladly accepted. Within an hour we had cooked not only noodles but also some chicken and vegetables for our lunch. We both had a great time, too. I felt like a child playing house in that tiny kitchen, and David relaxed and started making notes of supplies and gadgets he thought he might like to have. It was a huge turning point for him.

However, he still proceeded much more slowly than seemed necessary. Each time I felt upset that things weren't moving faster, I had to remind myself to immerse my world in love, to manage my thoughts, and to embrace reality instead of fighting it. I kept praying for guidance about how I could best support David. It took several weeks, but eventually he mustered the courage to call and set up appointments with Vocational Rehab and with his therapist.

Just before Christmas, David's caseworker told him she was arranging for him to have a more extensive evaluation which would include testing for autism. For this evaluation, I was asked to write a detailed summary of his life and to complete two lengthy questionnaires about his experiences and behaviors, past and present. It was valuable exercise for me to review his life.

When David went in for the appointment he was somewhat agitated, but the therapist quickly put him at ease and David found the experience quite fascinating. Within a few weeks he received an email with the results of this second evaluation. The first page said he had been diagnosed with severe anxiety, OCD, moderate autism, PTSD, and depression. It also said he demonstrated symptoms of other disorders.

As we read through the twelve-page report together, I began to see David in a different light. No wonder he'd had such a hard time developing a career path! He seemed so normal in so many ways, but his mind was always at war, struggling to fit into a world he often perceived as confusing, too noisy, too fast-paced, and deeply threatening.

As in earlier years, I was tempted to slip into the "whys" and the "what-ifs": "Why didn't I recognize this before?" "What if we had realized he needed help while he was in elementary school or even high school? Surely he wouldn't have been stuck in our basement all these years!"

Instead of going down those fruitless paths, I have done my best to rely on my stepping stones to joy. They have been priceless in helping me trust God and maintain a healthy perspective throughout this turbulent time.

# 20

# JOYFUL IN ANY KIND OF WEATHER

*Relying on my stepping stones to joy*

So now we have embarked on a whole new adventure. David meets regularly with therapists and others who are working to help him capitalize on his strengths and minimize his challenges. However, this adventure still requires a lot of my focused energy, and sometimes, a huge chunk of my day. Many of my unfinished projects continue to be on hold. I can only imagine how frustrated I would be if I were still trapped in those endless cycles of fear and perfectionism.

Although I have no way of knowing how things are going to work out, I am certain of God's pure, amazing, incomprehensible love for David. And I know He has that same beautiful love for me. This sure knowledge allows me to wake up each morning filled with hope, optimism, and trust.

To an outside observer, my life today may not appear to be much different from my life all those years ago. Of course, I've advanced from Mommy to Grammy, but I still live in the same house, attend the same church, enjoy many of the same activities, adore my family, and delight in many of the same friendships. If you were to ask people who have known me over the years, they would probably tell you I'm the same friendly person they've always known.

However, my life feels wonderfully, beautifully, joyfully different to me. Because of the amazing stepping stones God led me to discover throughout my journey, the shadows of fear and perfectionism don't have the same power to dominate my heart and mind as they once did. I can move forward trusting that God is in the details of my life, just as He is in the details of the lives of each of His children.

I am convinced He can take anything and turn it to our good if we will only let Him. He doesn't hold our past against us. He is there to teach us and lift us. He doesn't expect us to run faster than we have strength, but He does encourage us to be diligent. I think He takes particular delight in rewarding our diligent efforts to live more joyfully. Sometimes He helps us find strength we didn't know we had. Sometimes He gives us insights we desperately need. Often He blesses us with increased understanding and peace.

Perhaps the greatest gift I have received in my journey is the understanding that God loves me just as I am, right in this very moment even with all my flaws and faults and perfectionism and everything. It frees me to not only accept but to actually embrace who I am. That doesn't make me a narcissist or an egoist as I had once feared. But it does help me quiet those critical voices in my head so I can hear the whisperings of God's voice.

Since my greatest desire is to trust God and live in His love, whenever I find myself losing my footing in one of life's storms—feeling like I'm somehow not enough or that I need to be more in control—I turn to my stepping stones as quickly as possible. They are solid and unfailing. They have the power to break the shackles of fear and perfectionism and lift me above the clouds that obscure my view and distort my thinking.

When I notice some conflict or chaos I have created, those critical voices usually jump in trying to persuade me I'm hopeless or unlovable. But I know the truth, and I have developed a ready response to them. "Yep! I know I'm a mess! It's a good thing God loves messes!" This response helps me keep my perspective and frees me to move forward instead of cycling down into the dark pit of self-criticism. It's not always easy to dismiss those voices, but I have tools that work and I know how to use them.

Those tools help me when I am dealing with other kinds of challenges as well. Whether it's something as heavy as my doctor telling me I have cancer, or as inconvenient as a four-week delay in our remodel, or as disappointing as my daughter's family having to cancel a long-anticipated visit, as soon as I turn to my stepping stones I can feel God's loving hand leading me back to peace and joy.

God understands the ever-changing storms that come into each of our lives. He wants to help us navigate them so we can live joyfully. But we can only soar above the clouds when we discover and use the tools He offers us—tools which have the power to unchain the shackles that bind us down.

For me, and for many others who have shared their stories with me, these shackles come in the shadowy form of fear and perfectionism. They can show up any time, any place. They can be so subtle we don't recognize them for what they are, and so deeply entwined in our thinking that we are powerless to break them.

But God is eager to help us release our shackles and walk our individual paths with a heart full of joy. And because of His wondrous love, we don't have to be "perfect"—or anywhere close to perfect—to walk in the light of His love. He walks right beside us and blesses even our tiniest baby steps.

He is the way to joy. Living in His love is joy!

# MY STEPPING STONES TO JOY

*12 Tools for Managing Perfectionism and Living Joyfully*

1. Immerse the World in Love. *The foundation of all stepping stones.*
2. Establish a Relationship of Trust with God. *He's got your back.*
3. Manage Your Thoughts. *Don't believe everything you think!*
4. Embrace Reality. *Going to war with reality is a battle you can never win.*
5. Cultivate and Express Gratitude. *A powerful go-to for a quick change of heart.*
6. Live in the Present. *Life happens in this very moment. Don't miss it!*
7. Use the Law of Attraction. *Your thoughts and feelings will bring more of the same.*
8. Observe and Ask Questions. *Discover what lies beyond the obvious.*
9. Love Your Body. *It will love you back.*
10. Harbor No Secrets. *Reach out when you need help, even if you are afraid to.*
11. Forgive Freely. *Forgiveness is a gift of freedom only you can give yourself.*
12. Keep a Sense of Humor. *Life is too important to be taken seriously!*

You can read more of my thoughts and stories about the power of these stepping stones in my upcoming book, *Stepping Stones to Joy: 12 Tools for Managing Perfectionism and Living Joyfully.*

# ABOUT THE AUTHOR

Elona K. Shelley is a perfectionist in remission. She loves to encourage others who are struggling to maintain their sanity in a world that seems to say you are never enough. Elona is the author of *Confessions of a Molly Mormon*, a book which contrasts her relationship with her religion before and after she learned to recognize and manage her perfectionistic tendencies. She and her husband, Monte, raised their family in Orem, Utah where they now joyfully celebrate love and life with their adult children and their wonderful gaggle of grandchildren.

You can find more of Elona's writing at www.ElonaShelley.com.

18123769R00122

Made in the USA
San Bernardino, CA
28 December 2018